MARE MORTUUM, SALSUM
sive SALIS, LACUS ASPHALTITIS

Olim vallis Salinarum, prædicatæ fœcunditatis &
Post autem Sodoma eversa, mutata est in illan
qua hodie conspicitur. Divinæ ultionis admiranda

Adama

Sodoma

Gomorra

rhæi
Mephaath
Ar oen
Bamoth vallis
Abarim mons
Abyla Sisanij
Nain
Nebo
Beth. Peon
Callirrhœ
Mons Pisga
M. Nebo
Macherunta
Alexandria
Sittim
Bethabara

Zegor Engadi mons
Massada
Vallis benedictionis
Bethabara
S. Saba
Desertum Maon
Carmelus Mons
Medyn
Coena
Zyph
Loche

Hetæi
Galgala
Fons Helisei
Herodium
Quarentana mons
Cyprum
Iheric
Adonim
IUDAEA

Dooch
Aphara
Scharim
Phasele
Tribus
Desertum Adomin
Bethulia castrum
Tecua
Esthemoa
Sachak
Afar Santamar
Ain Bedlenim

Bethauen
Mijchmas
Terra rossa
Lapis Behon
Fons Solis
Gethsmani
Vallis Iosaphat
Ader
Sinæi
Amam
Capella S. Nicolai

Ennon
Bethel Rimom
Luza
Benjamin
Bahurim
Astaroth
Bethania
Olivarum mons
Bethsura
Bethlehem
Sepulchru Beth
Loth
Gilo
Hadassa
Maon
Gedera
Carmel

Montes Ephraim
Rama
Ceslon
Ariototh
Giah
Bahurim
Sion m.
Siloe fons
Sepulchru Rachel
Bezeth
Tribus Iuda
Rama
Arab
Dabyr
Cariath Sephar
Thamna
Enaim
Haz

Napolos
Fons Iacob
Caon
Gabaan
Sarilis
Hierusalem
Goliath m.
Kabreel
Bethzacha
Vallis Mambre
Enachim
Gerar
Sophor cast.
Gibilena

Mons Ga:
Bira, Ca:
phira
Iebusæi
Socoth
Iuda
Montana Iu:
dea. Etain
Hebron, Cariath
Arba
Tribus Simeon
Ccila

Gazer
Mons Hebal
Templu Iovis
Bethoron fu:
perior
Bethoron inferior
S. Phi
lippi
Escra
Saria
Chebbon
Bersabe
Betgebrim

Labana
Lemna
Macedo
Beroth
Emaus Nico: polis
Sophin
Botri
Raphaim Valli
Arechō
Escra
Ieblon
Irsames
Cænob. S. Ioãs
Herma

Asan
Bethsemes
Beth Da: gon
Baala
Cariath Iarim
Sina
Bethorim
Modin
Thimna
Nair
Adassa
Bethlebaoth
Sicleg
Castellum Abrahæ

Bala
Thamna
Azecha
Eglom
Fontana
Sepulch. Machab.
Jerimoth
Eslaol
Helcholad
Molada
S. Samuel
Arma
Bala

Lachis
Tebbon
Beth Nobe vel Bethnopolis
Chens
Cessalon
Azoti, sive
Adolam
Taph
Gaza

Sciroha
Lidda, vel Diospolis
Betfames
Geth, Gibelim
Eluzeropolis Gabathon
Saraba
Asco
Bethum haboth

Saurona
Senir mons
Rhamathaim Rhama, & Rhamula Saron M.
Iamnia Iude: oru portus
Caphar
Dan
Taphua
Ascalon

Joppe n. Iaffu
Castrum Beroaldi
Azotus, sive Assod
Acaron

Philis:
thijm

IDUMAEA PERIO

IDUM

Angaris mons

JESUS

JESUS

WHERE IT ALL BEGAN

by **GERALD BUSHELL**

PHOTOGRAPHY BY DAVID HARRIS

GENERAL EDITOR MORDECAI RAANAN

ABELARD-SCHUMAN NEW YORK

First United States Publication 1975
Abelard-Schuman, 666 Fifth Avenue, New York, N.Y. 10010

Copyright © 1970, 1975 by Nateev Ltd. P.O.Box 6048, Tel-Aviv, Israel

Library of Congress Cataloging in Publication Data

Bushell, Gerard, 1915–   . Jesus: where it all began.
Adaptation of In the Footsteps of Jesus, by W. E. Pax.
SUMMARY: Details the life of Jesus using historical
and literary allusions and photographs of the Holy Land.
1. Jesus Christ — Biography. 2. Palestine — Description and travel — Views.
3. Shrines — Palestine.
I. Pax, Wolfgang E. In the Footsteps of Jesus
II. Harris, David, fl. 1967–   illus. III. Title.
BT301.2.P382B87 1974   232.9'01   74–9373

ISBN: 0-200-00144-2

Published simultaneously in Canada by Fitzhenry & Whiteside Limited, Toronto

Printed in Israel by Peli Printing Works, Ltd., Givatayim, Israel

CONTENTS

CHAPTER 1 THE HOLY LAND AND THE HOLY CITY

*In which the regions where Jesus walked are
described*

People who seek God visit many holy places in the world, but there is really only *one* Holy Land, the Land of Israel. Over and over, God has revealed himself in this Land, to guide men and women to live according to his commandments. Why this Land should have been chosen is God's secret. Geographically and historically, it is a corridor between two continents, and this means movement and unrest. Perhaps this is God's way of telling mankind that, though hidden, he is still the Lord of life, the focal point of light and peace amid the seemingly insuperable hardships to which people are subjected. From this point of view the Holy Land is for all of us both a pattern and a parable. Its call to peace rings out as a vital challenge from a distant past, which cannot be ignored even today.

From the top of the Mount of Olives there is a view of the city of Jerusalem, often destroyed in the past, and always rebuilt. It looks petrified, yet its narrow streets and alleyways are teeming with life. This is the City of David, formerly the political capital of the Hebrew people. Above all, it has always been, and still is, their great religious center. The prophet

Ezechiel calls it "the hub of the earth" (5:5). The psalmist praises it as the mother of mankind (87:6). Isaiah tells about the royal feast which the Lord will prepare for his people on Mount Zion at the Messiah's coming when "the Lord God will wipe away tears from all faces" (25:8).

Through Jerusalem's calm air the sound of bells is heard from many churches. Their harmony seems to echo Jesus' final words on earth, "And lo, I am with you always, to the close of the age" (Matthew 28:20). It is a mystery why through Jesus, the Land of Israel was chosen for the second time as the setting for God's great revelation. The Land cannot be imagined without Jesus, as his life came to its very climax in Jerusalem. Luke, the evangelist, born elsewhere and of a foreign parentage, realized earlier and more clearly than other writers that, ultimately, Jerusalem was to be Jesus' final goal. He, therefore, describes Jesus' triumphal entry (on what we call Palm Sunday) as the beginning of messianic times. The joyful crowd cries out, "Blessed is the king who comes in the name of the Lord! Peace in heaven and glory in the highest!" (19:38).

> ## "...the angel Gabriel was sent from God to a city of Galilee named Nazareth"
> (Luke 1:26)

Nazareth is Christianity's most holy town. Climbing the foothills of lower Galilee, it has been called "Watchtower." Nestling in its own valley, it has been known also as the "Flower of Galilee". Here Christianity began, nearly two thousand years ago.

THE LIFE OF JESUS

It is difficult to write about the earthly existence of Jesus of Nazareth in accordance with modern historical methods. We know much more about his contemporaries, the Roman emperors Augustus and Tiberius, and about King Herod. Outside of brief notices in extrabiblical literature testifying to Jesus' existence, the most important material is provided by the Gospels. However, their authors were not concerned with producing a modern historical biography. They focused all their attention on the personality of the Lord.

As sometimes happens in an involvement with a well-loved person, his words and deeds were indelibly fixed in the memories of the apostles and the Gospel writers. Each of the evangelists saw Jesus through different eyes. They studied all aspects of his personality, always finding new traits yet unable to portray him fully, once and for all.

The Gospels, which have come down to us, were brought together slowly during the first century A.D.: stories of what he said and did, based on eyewitness accounts and retold in family circles. Then, these were assembled, in

11

The Church of the Annunciation (right), completed in 1969, is most modern in style. The massive block of its masonry symbolizes permanence, even eternity. Its dome opens like a flower over one of Christianity's most sacred spots, a cave (left), once part of a dwelling where, tradition says, Mary received heavenly news that she was to be Christ's mother.

accordance with certain theological viewpoints, for use in liturgy as teaching materials and as cathechism. As a rule, all the problems were considered from the Jewish point of view, but the writings were in Greek, the language of the Jews dispersed among the nations.

The life of Jesus is closely interwoven with the history of the country where he was born. His environment is well known to us, as a result of excavations carried out during the last few decades. Archaeology proves that the good tidings of the Gospel were not products of sheer fantasy, but were intimately related to real happenings in the world. In other words, the evangelists are narrating true facts, although we do have to bear in mind that archaeology has its limitations. There are no signposts, such as would be put up today, saying, "Jesus of Nazareth lived here."

Due to climatic conditions, earthquakes and the destruction of war, the outward appearance of many of these places has changed in the course of the centuries. What is even more decisive is the fact that, soon after Jesus died, the Holy Land was occupied by the Romans. They expelled both Jews and Christians, especially

from Jerusalem. State recognition of Christianity did not come until three hundred years later, under the emperor Constantine. In the fifth to the seventh centuries A.D., Christian life really flowered. Numerous pilgrims came from all parts of the world to visit the holy places and many churches were erected. With few exceptions, the most interesting archaeological finds date from this period. Some, however, are based on ancient traditions and serve to recall episodes in the life of Jesus. It is not really too important that some events actually took place in a spot different from the traditional one.

There is evidence of the way the Gospel was received by the faithful in the Byzantine churches, which are to be found even in the most remote corners of Samaria and Galilee. From the time of the Crusaders, practically every generation has paid homage to the holy places by adding new structures. Modern churches are deliberately designed to house ancient remains discovered by the excavators. This shows effectively their close relationship with the original buildings and the continuity of tradition through, at least, fifteen hundred years.

O favored one, the Lord is with you!'' (Luke 1:28)

The altars of the upper Church of the
Annunciation are offset by the huge mural
mosaic depicting the universal Christian Church.
On Christ's left are Peter and the apostles.
Groups in the lower right half of the
picture represent the hierarchy, those to
the left, the mass of the faithful.

The life of Jesus is brought home more closely when it is examined against the landscape of
the places where he actually lived. As the great
German poet Goethe put it, "If you want to
understand the poet you must visit his country." With some modification, these words are
never so apt as when applied to the Bible.

For instance, due to the climate, people in
the Middle East live predominantly outdoors.
Jesus, therefore, preached not only in the synagogue but also to crowds gathered on the hills,
in the fields, by the lake shore and in the market
place. The countryside impressed him deeply
and his parables reflect the kingdom of nature
which, to him, was symbolic of the supernatural world. In October, following the first rains,
the stony mountainsides suddenly bloom with
flowers, especially red poppylike anemones.
Immediately, one is confronted with the question of how there can be such lush growth
amid usual dryness and aridity. It is this wonder of nature which is reflected in Jesus' words,
"Consider the lilies of the field, how they grow,
they neither toil nor spin; yet I tell you, even
Solomon in all his glory was not arrayed like
one of these" (Matthew 6:28–29).

The desert is vast and solitary with its special play of colors when, toward evening, the shadows grow long, the sand turns a brilliant white and, finally, the sky — luminous with stars — arches above all. Only personal experience can make one realize that the wilderness is a place of salvation. It helps to explain how the Children of Israel acquired their religion during their wandering in the desert, and why Jesus withdrew into the wilderness for forty days of reflection and prayer. However, one must bear in mind another aspect of the desert — its dangers. Anyone who has had the experience of being deceived by a mirage — for instance, in the white heat of summer in the Jordan Valley — will appreciate how gravely Jesus must have been tempted when the devil "showed him all the kingdoms of the world and the glory of them; and he said to him, 'All these I will give you, if you will fall down and worship me'" (Matthew 4:8–9). Anyone who has been refreshed by the cool waters of a spring or a well, will realize the depth of meaning contained in the image of "living water" used by Jesus at Jacob's Well (John 4:10).

Above all, the Holy Land is the land of light. Anyone who has enjoyed the magnificent view of Jerusalem at sunrise or at sunset, or has seen airy, translucent clouds floating above the Mount of Olives, will appreciate why light has played such an important part in religious imagery. In line with constant references in the Bible and elsewhere in Hebrew ideology (e.g., at Qumran), Jesus could say of himself, "I am the light of the world" (John 8:12).

Jesus felt very close to other folk, and everyone who crossed his path was a brother, someone related to him. The Middle East changes slowly, and, to this day, one can meet the kind of people whom Jesus knew. The blind, in the Old City of Jerusalem, can still be seen going about in pairs, one leading the other. There are innumerable children in the alleys and squares. It was in defense of such youngsters that Jesus said, "Let the children come to me, and do not hinder them; for to such belongs the kingdom of heaven" (Matthew 19:14). Orthodox followers of Jewish piety still strive for salvation through faithful observance of all the commandments. Many such people were known in Jesus' time.

17

When Jesus walked through the market he must have known much the same atmosphere as today, the same merchandise (below), the same colors, the same smells. The Greek Catholic Church (right) by the market houses the ancient synagogue where Jesus is said to have gone to school.

In outlying districts, customs have changed even less than in the towns. This is especially true of areas inhabited by Arabs, off the beaten track of tourists. Weddings, for example, are still celebrated in the manner reflected in Jesus' parable of the ten virgins. The bridegroom comes at nightfall with torches and music to the house of his bride (Matthew 25:1). Hospitality, especially, is a sacred duty among these people, and Jesus must have known real warmth when he was invited into private homes.

CHAPTER 2 ORIGINS

In which the birth of Jesus is announced and takes place

"Jesus of Nazareth, the King of the Jews." With meticulous precision, Pilate mentioned Jesus' origins when writing the title for his cross. This was necessary as, at that time, "Jesus" was a common personal name, as judging by the discoveries of inscriptions. The home town is, therefore, designated to distinguish this Jesus from others. But Nazareth itself has become distinctive in history, as for a long time it was identified with Christ's followers. "Nazarene" meant "Christian". In fact, the latter title originated outside Palestine in the Syrian city of Antioch.

It is strange that Nazareth is not named either in the Old Testament or in the literature of the Talmud. Stranger still is that it is not mentioned by a profane writer such as Flavius Josephus, governor of Galilee and historian, who names practically every other town and settlement in the district, including Jotapata (Yodfat) very close by, and the neighboring Sepphoris. Nazareth must have been a lowly little place, which clarifies the patronizing remark of Nathaniel, "Can anything good come out of Nazareth?" (John 1:46).

Nazareth's geographical position would account for this. The ancient Via Maris (Highway by the Sea) linking Damascus and Egypt ran about six miles east of Mount Tabor into the plain of Jezreel, avoiding the foothills where Nazareth stood. Because the town really nestled in a mountain valley it was usually bypassed in ancient times. Nevertheless, it was inhabited early in history, as was the Carmel range across the plain. Excavations on the site of the basilica of Nazareth have revealed many grottos, wine and olive presses, silos and cisterns, all dating back to Herodian (Roman) times, indicating that the small population of the village lived mainly by farming. Houses with flat roofs were sometimes built in front of natural caves, the latter being used as storerooms or stables. Such dwellings may well have filled the valley, even at that time.

Nazareth, therefore, is truly historic ground, even though the settlement had no political significance, and might have been forgotten, in time. However, because this was the home town of Jesus, its name is famous throughout the modern world.

An event took place here which cannot be

understood at all unless it is approached with deep reverence. Luke reports it in detail, but without sensationalism. Precisely because of its simplicity, his account makes an impression, and it may well be based, ultimately, on what Mary of Nazareth herself had to tell.

THE ANNUNCIATION

"In the sixth month the angel Gabriel was sent from God to a city of Galilee named Nazareth, to a virgin betrothed to a man whose name was Joseph, of the house of David; and the virgin's name was Mary. And he came to her and said, 'Hail, O favored one, the Lord is with you!' But she was greatly troubled at the saying, and considered in her mind what sort of greeting this might be. And the angel said to her, 'Do not be afraid, Mary, for you have found favor with God. And behold, you will conceive in your womb and bear a son, and you shall call his name Jesus. He will be great, and will be called the Son of the Most High; and the Lord God will give to him the throne of his father David, and he will reign over the house of Jacob for ever; and of his kingdom there will be no end.' And Mary said to the angel, 'How can this be, since I have no husband?' And the angel said to her, 'The Holy Spirit will come upon you, and the power of the Most High will overshadow you; therefore the child to be born will be called holy, the Son of God. And behold, your kinswoman Elizabeth in her old age has also conceived a son; and this is the sixth month with her who was called barren. For with God nothing will be impossible.' And Mary said, 'Behold, I am the handmaid of the Lord; let it be to me according to your word.' And the angel departed from her."

God's voice is often dramatized in the Scriptures as a communication by an angel. Here, a young — about fifteen-year-old — Jewish maiden is being addressed. The greeting is full of implications to be considered against the background of Middle Eastern customs, where salutations take on many different forms. There is one suitable for man to man, one for acquaintances casually passed by on the street, another — reserved and formal — between persons who are not married. Here, the angel's "Ave" of the Greek Gospel is quite unusual and means, literally,

"In those days Mary arose and went with haste into the

Seeking further light on the mystery of the Annunciation, Mary hastened south into the hill country of Judah to the town of her kinswoman, Elizabeth. Tradition identifies the settlement as Ein Karem, now a suburb of Jerusalem.

'Rejoice' or 'Good cheer!' Mary, the maiden, is greatly disturbed and is promptly doubly reassured. First, she is told that she is full of grace: highly favored by God. The second assurance to her, "The Lord is with you," has profound meaning as we know from similar greetings throughout the Bible. Before great undertakings, Moses (Exodus 3:11), Joshua (Joshua 1:3–5) and David (2 Samuel 7:3) had been similarly encouraged: "for the Lord is with you." The greeting to Mary, therefore, implies a call to a most providential and far-reaching mission, changing history and affecting future generations.

Mary's mission of motherhood is then explained in detail. She is to bear the Messiah. Her son will be great, perfectly fulfilling the words spoken to her ancestor David: "Your house and your kingdom shall be made sure for ever before me; your throne shall be established for ever" (2 Samuel 7:16). This mention of motherhood is a supreme test for Mary. She had been brought up in the strict Jewish tradition and, therefore, had a deep respect for marriage. Moreover, she is already wedded to her husband, though they have not lived together. To Westerners this may seem strange, but those familiar with the Middle Eastern customs will know that the engagement itself implies a marriage contract, and unfaithfulness on the part of either party is a most grievous injury to the other. Mary's reaction is more than mere mystification. It is that of fear. "How can this be?"

Mary is further reassured. Nothing will happen to which her conscience can object. Like the cloud which filled the tabernacle, symbolizing the presence of God (Exodus 40:34), the Holy Ghost, God's creative power, will settle upon her and she will become another divine dwelling place in a most personal sense. In the Bible, many such extraordinary events are accompanied by a sign and a pledge. So Mary is told of a distant kinswoman's intimate secret about a similar unexpected pregnancy, providential in itself because nothing is impossible to God. With this appeal to God who is ever true, Mary consents and the history of Christianity begins.

Today, this solemn moment is commemorated in one of the greatest churches in the

ill country,. to a city of Judah ... and greeted Elizabeth"

(Luke 1:39–40)

world, the Basilica of the Annunciation, consecrated on March 23, 1969. The huge block of the stone edifice is a symbol of permanence, even of eternity, but the graceful cupola opens like a flower over the sacred spot where Mary's consent is remembered. Down through the spacious upper church, it throws light on age-old remains in the crypt where, earlier, a basilica had been erected in Byzantine times. There are relics which are older still: a pre-Byzantine synagogue-church, together with a baptismal font bearing many inscriptions. One is in Greek *X E MAPIA:* "Hail Mary." These and other items serve as evidence that Mary's motherhood was venerated in this place, at least as early as the second century A.D., that is, by the second generation of Christians.

The exact spot where the Annunciation took place cannot be determined. However, it is almost certain that it occurred in a small stone dwelling which may have soon disappeared, like so many others. It may have been situated in front of a natural cave, and it was to such a grotto — presently situated beneath the huge modern basilica — that

devotion to the mystery of the Annunciation was transferred.

Another tradition has it that God's voice came to Mary first near the village well, where she had gone to draw water. "And Mary took the pitcher and went forth to fill it with water: and to a voice saying, 'Hail, thou that art highly favored; the Lord is with thee: blessed art thou among women.' And she looked about her upon the right hand and upon the left, to see whence this voice should be: and being filled with trembling she went to her house and set down the pitcher and took the purple and sat down upon her seat and drew out the thread. And behold an angel of the Lord stood before her saying..." (Protoevangelium of James 11:1).

Nazareth still has one spring which has never run dry. Its waters now run under the Greek Orthodox Church of St. Gabriel (or of the Annunciation), then to a public outlet on the main Nazareth-Tiberias highway. But, in the past, the scene of womenfolk meeting here to gossip for a while and then carrying home their water jugs, balanced on their heads, created a charming sight. Mary's

Lord, and my spirit rejoices in God my Savior'" *(Luke 1:46–47)*

The courtyard of the Church of the Visitation, in Ein Karem. The *Magnificat* is inscribed in forty-one languages on the plaques on the wall at the rear. In this song Mary rejoiced that she was to be the mother of the Lord.

encounter with God could easily have taken place in this exact spot, but this tradition is too recent to warrant complete credibility.

Nazareth's mysteries of the Annunciation and Incarnation explain why Jesus was named, not after a father, but simply "Son of Mary." The inevitable accusations against her have arisen but, in this respect, even the Koran comes to her defense: "This was Jesus, the Son of Mary: the word is truth" (Sura 19:35).

However, because Joseph believed in the miraculous occurrence and took Mary as his wife, Jesus also became the "Son of David." In ancient times, questions of descent were determined according to the legal lineage of the father and were not determined exclusively by biological considerations. Since Jewish family tradition is generally accurate in the matter of genealogy, the descent of Joseph from David may be accepted as historically true. Joseph was a "just" man, a gentleman, who, like Bedouin notables today, may have lived in poverty, but whose bearing and mien manifested a dignity which could derive only from a splendid past.

25

"...(Elizabeth) exclaimed... 'why is this granted me that the mother of my Lord should come to me?'"

(Luke 1:42–43)

The mosaic on the facade of the Church of the Visitation shows Mary on her way from Nazareth to Elizabeth's home.

JESUS' BIRTH

The birth of Jesus, in about the year 7 B.C., was reported by Luke: "In those days a decree went out from Caesar Augustus that all the world should be enrolled. This was the first enrollment, when Quirinius was governor of Syria. And all went to be enrolled, each in his own city. And Joseph also went up from Galilee, from the city of Nazareth, to Judea, to the city of David, which is called Bethlehem, because he was of the house and lineage of David, to be enrolled with Mary, his betrothed, who was with child. And while they were there, the time came for her to be delivered. And she gave birth to her firstborn son and wrapped him in swaddling cloths, and laid him in a manger, because there was no place for them in the inn" (Luke 2:1–7).

This text, introduced by historical comments, reads almost like an official document. The birth is related to contemporary, well-known events, which lent it validity. From this we draw the obvious conclusion that Jesus was a real person. At the same time, it permits examination of the event, seemingly so unimportant, against the background of

27

"...henceforth all generations will call me blessed"

(Luke 1:48)

Frescoes and mosaics make the
Church of the Visitation the
gayest in the Holy Land.
Behind the altar, Mary
is seen in glory, venerated
by angels, Doctors of the
Church and saintly folk of
Christian history.

world history. Mention is made of the Roman emperor, and this is a reminder that from 63 B.C. onward the region belonged to the Roman Empire, being part of the province of Syria. Jews, however, were allowed special privileges and were largely left to manage their own affairs. Herod the Great, of mixed Idumaean and Jewish blood, had so ingratiated himself with the Romans that they made him a king. He was by no means popular with all the Jews and depended for security on Rome.

Augustus and Jesus — chance or design? Early Christian thinkers had already pondered the question of why these two great figures should have been contemporaries. Augustus, unlike any other emperor, was the most important ruler of antiquity. Following the political and social turmoil which had preceded him, the world saw him as the personification of its hopes for peace and lasting security. But, the *Pax Augusta* (peace imposed by the Emperor Augustus) was not limited only to the realm of politics. It was conceived as bringing peace to the whole world with a renewal of the universal order. Therefore, this ruler of mankind becomes "the savior" and

is called "Augustus": he who is worthy of reverence (as a god).

Augustus once expressed the wish to be the founder of "the optimum state," and hoped that the foundations laid by him would never be disturbed. Many years after he died, Philo, the famous Alexandrian Jewish philosopher, called him "the supreme benefactor." Mankind had reached the point of self-extermination. Augustus saved it and gave it a new direction. His greatest achievement was the *Pax Augusta* for which he is ever renowned. Yet, he had to confess that no human being can, by his own devices, achieve perfection. His hopes remained unfulfilled and, under his successors, his well-laid foundations crumbled.

His great counterpart, entirely unknown to him, was Jesus of Nazareth, whose kingdom was not of this world and who could yet claim, "On this rock I will build my church, and the powers of death shall not prevail against it" (Matthew 16:18). It was not by chance that Augustus and Jesus were contemporaries. They were complementary, in the sense that they represented two spiritual worlds. Ethelbert Stauffer, the well-known

29

New Testament scholar, has put it well: "Augustus displayed the capabilities and the limitations of the most perfect specimen of *Homo imperiosus* (ruler). That is the meaning of his story for the destiny of man. That is why his extreme achievements illuminate the enormous problems and the tragedy of historic events. Something is wrong with the history of the world. Something has to be put right, something must happen. We are faced with the problem which made history progress from Augustus to Jesus."

The immediate background of Jesus' birth in Bethlehem was the taking of a census. The Romans had an excellent system of administration, and an accurate assessment of tax levies was one of its main functions. Therefore, census taking was more than a mere counting of heads. It took place at regular intervals, and in each of the various provinces, was supervised by the governor through his legates. In the area of Bethlehem, the official legate may have been King Herod himself. The detailed method of registration is known literally from an Egyptian scroll of 104 A.D.: "Gaius Vibius Maximus, governor of Egypt,

The grotto at the northern end of the Church of St. John, Ein Karem, once formed part of the dwelling where Zechariah and Elizabeth are thought to have lived. A star under the altar marks the traditional spot of John the Baptist's birth.

"But his mother said,... 'he shall be called John'"

(Luke 1:60)

The pledge of Mary's future motherhood
was confirmed by Elizabeth, her cousin, who was,
at the time, herself expecting the birth
of her son, later known as John the Baptist.
The traditional locality where this occurred
is the garden town of Ein Karem, "Vineyard Spring."

proclaims: As we are about to take a census, it is necessary to order all those who are for any reason away from home to return to their own districts so that the census may be taken in the usual way." This applied to married women and all property, as well as the head of the family. Joseph probably owned property in Bethlehem and it was certainly the ancestral home of his family, the house of David.

BETHLEHEM

Unlike Nazareth, Bethlehem is frequently mentioned in the Bible. It lies in the hills, five miles south of Jerusalem. There Ruth gleaned barley. There David was shepherding flocks when he was called to be king. For the small town, the prophet Micah predicted a famous future: "But you, O Bethlehem Ephrathah, who are little to be among the clans of Judah, from you shall come forth for me one who is to be ruler of Israel, whose origin is from of old, from ancient days" (Micah 5:2). Christians have seen all this fulfilled in the world-wide fame which Bethlehem has always enjoyed among them.

The notion that, in Jesus' time, Bethlehem was an unknown village is far from true. Quite close to it passed the main road from Jerusalem to Gaza, via Hebron. The fact that it was a stopover for travelers is clear from the prophet Jeremiah who, about 587 B.C., mentions a caravansary — or inn — nearby (Jeremiah 41:17). This would have been a typical Middle Eastern *khan* (rest house): a rectangular wall surrounding an open space with a well, where animals were unharnessed and people rested on the ground.

About four miles to the east is the Herodium, an isolated hill on which Herod built his palace. At its foot was a town which could be reached only through Bethlehem. Since the Herodium was the administrative center for all places south of Jerusalem, this must have been a much-traveled route.

Typical of the district are weather-hewn caves, especially in the soft rock at the foot of cliff faces. Many of these have been enlarged and are even fronted by man-made houses. Today, they still serve as shelters for the Bedouins and their animals. As a local man, Joseph must have been familiar with such

33

> *"...Joseph also went up ... to Judea, to the city of David, which is called Bethlehem ... to be enrolled with Mary, his betrothed, who was with child"* *(Luke 2:4–5)*

caves on the eastern slope of the town, close to the pastures. And in such a cave Jesus was born.

The usual explanation of how this came about is that there was no accommodation for Joseph and Mary in the travelers' inn. A less picturesque, but perhaps a more realistic concept is that Joseph and Mary retired from the more elaborate room, which served as living quarters for his family and relatives, probably more numerous at census time. They went to the cave stable in the rear, simply because the normal sleeping quarters was "no place for them" at this critical time of imminent birth. (There are several practical reasons to believe this to be true, the most valid being the fact that Luke mentions here, not the technical term for "inn" as in Luke 10:34, but a word he himself uses later on for "upper room" (Luke 22:11). In the Bethlehem reference, this latter would mean the living quarters, higher and separate from the cave stable.)

As in other instances, a specific grotto became associated with a sacred memory, in this case that of Jesus' birth. In the fourth

Bethlehem enshrines the grotto-stable where Jesus was born. The Holy Family settled here after moving from Nazareth. Here Joseph was called upon to register them during a Roman census, possibly because he had property there, certainly because he was of the family of David and Bethlehem was David's town.

"O Bethlehem... from you shall come a ruler who will govern my people Israel"

(Matthew 2:6)

The towers of Bethlehem's skyline
proclaim it sacred to different faiths
and denominations. They mark
a Latin church in the Basilica of the
Nativity; a Greek Orthodox Community;
a mosque; a Greek Catholic church;
the Armenian Orthodox Community and the
Lutheran church.

century, Constantine built above it a basilica with five naves, the oldest Christian church. The cave has been altered, in the course of time, but its outline still preserves the original shape: two chambers, one on a higher level than the other. The higher chamber was for human habitation; the lower one served as a storeroom and a stable. Actually, not a great number of animals could have been accommodated, so that the ox and the ass of medieval Christmas scenes are an embellishment. Nowadays, one regrets the artificial marble and asbestos coverings on the walls, but here and there the bare rock shows through, especially on the roof, conveying some idea of how the grotto looked originally.

The apocryphal Gospel of James has vivid descriptions of the daily life of the people at that time. In connection with the Nativity, it tells that Mary's labor pains began on the road shortly before she and Joseph reached Bethlehem, so Joseph lifted her from the ass and carried her into a grotto. To preserve this memory, in the fifth century, Christians erected a church there called Kathisma, "Mary's Rest," and this came to embody

The Basilica of the Nativity, like an ancient fortress, has withstood the ravages of time and war, standing intact since the early sixth century. The single, low entrance is pictured on the left hand side.

many of Bethlehem's memories. The church has long since disappeared.

The birth probably occurred during the season following the early rains, when the soil is softened and new growth is seen. In the fertile fields around Bethlehem, shepherds were tending their flocks. To them came the first news of Jesus' birth. God's voice reached them through an angel: "Behold, I bring you good news of great joy which will come to all the people; for to you is born this day in the city of David a Savior, who is Christ the Lord". (Luke 2:10–11). When a Bedouin woman gives birth to a child, her female relatives, still today, tell the husband waiting outside the tent: "We bring you good news of a great joy, for to you is born this day...." Equally rooted in ancient traditions is the angels' song of praise. In structure it derives from age-old Jewish liturgy and is now recited every Sunday morning at the Latin Mass: "Gloria in excelsis Deo": "Glory to God in the highest, and on earth peace among men with whom he is pleased!" (Luke 2:14).

In the fourth century, a church and a very large monastery were built, in what is known as Shepherds' Field. Nearby are numerous cisterns and caves which were used by shepherds. A beautiful modern chapel is tent-shaped, lit through windows of dark blue, in contrast to the clear soft white light flooding down from the dome with its myriad of little windows. This is a symbol of the night-sky scene suddenly outshone by the glory from the heavens. From Shepherds' Field there is a magnificent view of Bethlehem to which the shepherds hastened, as soon as the angel had spoken to them. This again is in keeping with a popular Middle Eastern custom by which neighbors and acquaintances visit the home of a newborn baby to offer traditional congratulations.

CHAPTER 3 JESUS' EARLY LIFE

*In which various incidents indicate his future
importance*

Following the story of the Nativity, Luke reports two important events: the circumcision of Jesus, and the purification of Mary. "And at the end of eight days, when he was circumcised, he was called Jesus, the name given by the angel before he was conceived in the womb. And when the time came for their purification according to the law of Moses, they brought him up to Jerusalem to present him to the Lord (as it is written in the law of the Lord, 'Every male that opens the womb [firstborn son] shall be called holy to the Lord') and to offer a sacrifice according to what is said in the law of the Lord, 'a pair of turtledoves, or two young pigeons'." (Luke 2:21–24).

These two ceremonies are reported simply as facts and give further proof that the Holy Family faithfully observed Jewish traditions, many of which are in use to this day. Circumcision, practiced generally in the Middle East, was given deep religious significance by the Israelites as the outward sign of the covenant made between God and Abraham (Genesis 17:10). After the Jews were dispersed throughout the world, circumcision became their

especially distinguishing mark. At the ceremony of circumcision, the infant receives its name, often one formerly borne by a deceased member of the family. This custom was universal, and helps to explain the surprise of Elizabeth's friends when she insisted that her son be named John: "None of your kindred is called by this name" (Luke 1:61). Jesus, likewise, received a name which God alone had chosen for him.

Luke also mentions purification. According to law, a Jewish woman who had given birth was considered unclean for forty days, forbidden to leave the house or touch any holy object. At the end of this period, she had to journey to Jerusalem to be pronounced clean by the high priest on duty at the Gate of Nicanor leading to the temple. Poor people had to sacrifice a pair of turtledoves, and the rich had to make the additional sacrifice of a year-old lamb. Moreover, the firstborn was consecrated to the service of God by his being "presented at the temple." Since, however, there was a special caste charged with religious service (the Levites), the boy was ransomed back to ordinary life through the

Christ, Mary and John the Baptist are represented in a medieval fresco which decorates the Chapel of the Tower in the Basilica of the Nativity.

payment of five shekels. Luke omits reference to this because, for him, Jesus was irrevocably consecrated to the service of his heavenly Father.

On this occasion, the Holy Family met an old man, Simeon, who exclaimed with prophetic joy: "Lord, now lettest thou thy servant depart in peace, according to thy word: for mine eyes have seen thy salvation which thou hast prepared in the presence of all peoples, a light for revelation to the Gentiles, and for glory to thy people Israel" (Luke 2:29–32).

They also met an elderly lady, called Anna. Seeing the child, she too praised God and gave thanks. Here we should remember that, in the Middle East, old people are held in high esteem because of their great wisdom and insight. Anna is actually called a prophetess, not to designate any special office, but to draw attention to her dignity and devotion to God.

Joseph did not lead his family back to Nazareth immediately, possibly because he intended to settle permanently in Bethlehem. He would have lived in a small stone dwelling,

Steps to the right lead down to the
Manger in the Grotto of the Nativity. The
altar (right) commemorates the visit
of the Wise Men who adored the child Jesus.

"...she gave birth to her first-born son... laid him in a

The silver star marks the spot where
the Nativity is said to have occurred. The
fifteen lamps which surround it, were
donated by various Christian communities.

manger, because there was no place... in the inn" *(Luke 2:7)*

Floor mosaics took the place of carpets in early Christian Churches. This fifth-century design in Bethlehem's basilica reflects the agricultural interests of the faithful: apples, grapes and pomegranates.

but of this no trace remains — unless, as suggested above, the grotto of the Nativity was his own property.

One further feature of the infancy story may be stressed. In the Middle East, much attention is paid to the suckling of babies. The Arabs have a saying: "The milk will act on the character; a boy who has had plenty of mother's milk has a strong character, his head full of his mother's milk." Mothers frequently nurse their children for two or three years — as is illustrated by the story of Hannah and her son Samuel, who, as soon as he was weaned, began to help with religious services (1 Samuel 1:22, 24; 2:11).

Not far from the Basilica of the Nativity in Bethlehem, there is the so-called Milk Grotto. Legend has it that, while Mary was nursing her child, a few drops of milk fell on the rocks and turned them white. Through the centuries, pilgrims have taken home small pieces of the rock, as the chalk is believed to have miraculous powers. Even today, prayerful Moslems and Christians carry home a fragment, grind it and mix it with the food of nursing mothers to encourage the flow of

The main event at Christmas time in the Holy Land is the annual midnight Mass in the Latin Church of St. Catherine. Thousands of pilgrims from all over the world gather for the ceremony.

natural milk. The story about Mary is probably legendary but, again, it is well founded in local custom and stresses Mary's loving care for her child.

THE WISE MEN

A further major incident connected with Jesus' infancy is the story of the visit to Bethlehem of wise men from the east. "Now when Jesus was born in Bethlehem of Judea in the days of Herod the king, behold, wise men from the East came to Jerusalem saying, 'Where is he who has been born king of the Jews? For we have seen his star in the East, and have come to worship him.' When Herod the king heard this, he was troubled, and all Jerusalem with him" (Matthew 2:1–3). He questioned the chief priests and the scribes as to where the Messiah might have been born, and received the answer: "in Bethlehem."

So the king sent the wise men there, ordering them to report back to him on whatever they might find out. "When they had heard the king they went their way; and lo, the star which they had seen in the East

went before them, till it came to rest over the place where the child was. When they saw the star, they rejoiced exceedingly with great joy; and going into the house they saw the child with Mary his mother, and they fell down and worshiped him. Then, opening their treasures, they offered him gifts, gold and frankincense and myrrh" (Matthew 2:9–11).

This story has to be viewed as part of traditional ceremonial greetings which follow a birth, accompanied by the giving of small presents. Many friends and strangers have already paid their respects, and those who do not pay such a visit are considered guilty of insult. The simple shepherds come, as do these foreigners from afar, but the official representatives of the Jewish people, the king and his counselors, stay away. Consequently the evangelist Matthew, quite early in his gospel, deduces that people are divided about Jesus' status, right from the time of his early childhood. Lowly folk and Gentiles accept him, but he is not acknowledged by his own people.

There has been much speculation as to who these wise men were. Justin, born in Nablus,

"And in that region there were shepherds out in the field, keeping watch over their flock by night" (Luke 2 :8)

Bethlehem is adequately supplied with water. Its lush fields (below) provide pasture for flocks as in David's time. Shepherds pasturing their flocks were the first to know that Jesus was born in Bethlehem. A large fresco (right) in Shepherds' Field chapel shows the angel bringing the good tidings that the Messiah has been born.

Among the many archaeological finds in Shepherds' Field are remains of a Byzantine farm connected with a church and monastery which commemorated the angel's message.

Samaria (c. 150 A.D.), was positive that they came from "Arabia," which, for him, meant Transjordan, where the Nabataeans lived. As is evident from archaeological finds in this region, people at that time were greatly interested in astrology. Among the Nabataeans, small Jewish communities lived in exile, and conflicting theories as to the coming of the Messiah must have been known to the Gentile population. Furthermore, the fact that Transjordanian traditions were known in Jerusalem itself is obvious from funerary inscriptions found on the Mount of Olives. A visit by notables of Transjordan to Bethlehem, therefore, is quite conceivable, on historical grounds. Moreover, Christian tradition has always been fascinated by the story of these dignitaries who came unassumingly to worship the child Jesus.

As for the star the wise men saw, legend has it that it vanished into the large well near the grotto of the Nativity, and that only the pure of heart can still see it there. There must have been a long tradition behind this famous well, as the Crusaders knew about its being a distinctive feature of Bethlehem.

"A woman in the crowd... said to him, 'Blessed is the womb that bore you, and the breasts that you sucked!'"

(Luke 11:27)

Fearful of Herod who sought to take the life of the child Jesus, the Holy Family was forced to flee from Bethlehem to Egypt. This bas-relief of Mary nursing her infant can be seen in the Milk Grotto, Bethlehem.

In Luke's narrative of the infancy of Jesus, Augustus is the key figure of reference. In Matthew's account, it is Herod. This raises another question: Herod and Jesus, chance or design? Between the two personalities a greater contrast would hardly have been possible. Herod had used slave labor to build himself a magnificent palace, the Herodium, overlooking the Bethlehem skyline. Rivaling Pompeii in its magnificence, its ruins even today testify to the presumptuous character of the monarch who built it. As indicated by his other fortress, Machaerus, to the east of the Dead Sea, Herod himself seems to have lived on the fringe of civilization. He descended from the desert country of Idumaea; yet, with his Hellenistic-Roman upbringing, he sought continually to be accepted as a man of the world. He even had religious pretensions, and his reputation as a builder of Jewish places of worship was surpassed only by Solomon, centuries before. Personally, he was a very unhappy man, suspicious even of his own family, and ruthless in executing those whom he mistrusted. Perhaps the biographical note about him in the apocryphal Assumption of

Moses does not altogether exaggerate: "There followed a bold king, not descendant from a priestly family, who was presumptuous and wicked. He killed old and young, and the whole country was terribly afraid of him. He ravaged the people with slaughter, as had happened in Egypt." (6:22).

All this is reflected in the brief Gospel story of Herod's plot to do away with the child Jesus. "Then Herod, when he saw that he had been tricked by the wise men, was in a furious rage, and he sent and killed all the male children in Bethlehem and in all that region who were two years old or under, according to the time which he had ascertained from the wise men" (Matthew 2:16–17).

Matthew (2:18) completes the story of this tragedy by referring to Rachel (who died near Bethlehem) mourning in her tomb for descendants herded together and driven off into exile (Jeremiah 31:15), crying again for another lost generation. Implicitly, however, he would insinuate (like Jeremiah before him: 31:17) that there was reason to hope that under a new leader "your children shall come back to their own country."

EXILE IN EGYPT

A story of exile into the unknown follows immediately. In a dream, Joseph heard the voice of God through an angel: "Rise, take the child and his mother and flee to Egypt, and remain there till I tell you; for Herod is about to search for the child and destroy him" (Matthew 2:13). At that time Egypt, governed directly from Rome, was a recognized place of refuge. It had numerous Jewish communities, some of them quite large. The Gospel record does not mention the locality where the Holy Family took refuge, but tradition has it that it was Heliopolis, north of Cairo. A crypt beneath the Church of St. Sergius there, dating from the sixth century, is usually pointed out as their dwelling place.

There has always been a close connection between the land of the Nile and Palestine and it was confirmed by this flight of the Holy Family. The journey, to Egypt and back, down through the Negev (Southland) and across the Sinai Desert, must have been extremely difficult. A similar journey was once made out of Egypt by the Chosen People under the leadership of Moses, and the significance of Jesus' return is emphasized by Matthew. Like another Moses, Jesus comes back to the Holy Land to fulfill a mission of salvation, in accordance with the plans of Providence: "Out of Egypt I have called my son" (Matthew 2:15).

Joseph led his little family back to Israel, but he had to seek a new home again, not near Jerusalem, but far to the north in Galilee: "But when he heard that Archelaus reigned over Judea in place of his father Herod, he was afraid to go there, and being warned in a dream, he withdrew to the district of Galilee. And he went and dwelt in a city called Nazareth" (Matthew 2:22–23).

These terse words reflect faithfully the political history of the country. Augustus divided Herod's kingdom among his three surviving sons. Archelaus received his father's southern domains, Judaea, Samaria and Jerusalem; Antipas — always called Herod by the evangelists, and not to be confused with his forebear — was appointed ruler of Galilee, becoming Jesus' new overlord; Philip reigned farther north, in the area now known as the Golan Heights, his lasting monument being the town of Caesarea Philippi, today called Baniyas.

Joseph and his family probably traveled north, along the Mediterranean coast, as far as Caesarea. Then they would have had to turn east to cross the plain of Jezreel, and so reach Nazareth. On this last stage of the journey they would have been exposed to the sight of the great Carmel range, celebrated for its beauty even in Old Testament times (Song of Solomon 7:5). Various legends have it that they stopped for the night, either in a cave near Atlit or in the so-called Cave of the Prophets at the foot of Carmel. Often, behind such stories lies an important religious reference. Undoubtedly, in this case, it is the stress on the New Testament connection between Jesus and Elijah, the prophet of Mount Carmel and the precursor of the Messiah in Jewish traditional belief. In the same Cave of the Prophets, Moslems, too, have worshiped Elijah since ancient times. And so, today, the place, in its neat little garden, reflects the ecumenical spirit espoused by Jesus, concerned as he was with the whole of mankind.

RETURN TO NAZARETH

Jesus lived in Nazareth for thirty years. While the apocryphal books try to fill this period will all kinds of detail, the four Gospels are almost silent on the subject. This was the prelude to his public appearance, when he attracted a great deal of attention by his words and deeds, all culminating in his death and resurrection. With due respect, we will try to penetrate this silence a little, in order to appreciate more fully what happened subsequently.

Luke reports, "And the child grew and became strong, filled with wisdom; and the favor of God was with him" (2:40). We can assume that the natural development of the boy Jesus was similar to that of many other children. Like other youngsters in the Middle East, he had a firm place within the family. Even on official occasions, there is always mention of three members of this household, so that Joseph, Mary and Jesus represented a closely-knit unit. However, they were part of a much larger family group or clan, which also includes the "brothers and sisters" mentioned in the Gospels. In accordance with Oriental usage, they may have been cousins, more or less closely related (Hebrew had no distinct word for our "cousin"). The most important relatives were Mary's cousin Elizabeth and her husband, the priest Zechariah, parents of John the Baptist. Immediately after the Annunciation, Mary visited Elizabeth, who showed deep insight into the joyous mystery Mary was experiencing: "Blessed are you among women, and blessed is the fruit of your womb! And why is this granted me, that the mother of my Lord should come to me?" (Luke 1:42–43). Mary answered with the famous song of praise, the Magnificat: "My soul magnifies the Lord!..." (Luke 1:46–55).

The meeting of the two women represents a deep harmony in ardor and faith and, at the same time, shows the closeness of the relationship between the two cousins. According to Luke, this took place about five miles from Jerusalem, in an ancient town in the hill district of Judah. From ancient Christian times, it has been identified as Ein Karem. The present village rests picturesquely within enfolding hills and is reminiscent of some Italian township with its many monasteries

"...(Joseph) took the child and his mother... and departe

and churches. The Church of St. John the Baptist, with the grotto where he was born, dates from the Byzantine period and is surrounded by remains of a settlement from Herodian (Roman) times. On the slopes of the western hill, near the town spring, is the Church of the Visitation. It has its own well in the crypt, and there are definite indications of the existence of a building in Byzantine times.

That Joseph and Mary's families were fairly extensive can be deduced also from the historical fact that some descendants were still living around Nazareth in the third century. At his trial in Asia Minor, under Decius, the martyr Konon confessed: "I come from the town of Nazareth in Galilee; I am related to Christ and in serving him I am following the tradition of my family." In the lower church of the Basilica of the Annunciation, a fine mosaic, from the fifth century, is still to be seen. It bears the inscription: "From the deacon Konon in Jerusalem." It is evident that the donor wished to honor his namesake (and perhaps his own relative) in this manner.

The route from Israel to Egypt crosses the Sinai desert, an area of never-ending wilderness and heat. Sometimes roads penetrate red granite mountain gorges.

> Egypt, and remained there until the death of Herod"
>
> *(Matthew 2:14–15)*

GROWING UP

Joseph was an artisan and, though the Gospels do not say so directly, it is highly probable that Jesus served as an apprentice under him. According to the Talmud, a father is obliged not only to support his son but also to teach him a trade. The distinction we make between ecclesiastical and secular occupations did not exist in Jesus' time. On the contrary, boys studying the Jewish Law were expected to learn some skill. Paul, for instance, was a tentmaker. As craftsmen often had to travel about in search of work, Jesus would have had an opportunity to get to know Nazareth and its citizens with all their problems, needs, weaknesses and faults. Where exactly Joseph had his home, we do not know. However, caves, cisterns, silos and winepresses under the present Church of St. Joseph in Nazareth, give a vivid idea of how people of the time lived, even though we cannot connect them with certainty to Joseph's house or workshop.

Of greater importance is the religious environment in which Jesus grew up. There must have been a group of devout Jews in Nazareth, and Jesus' family would have belonged to it. During the excavations at Caesarea, a fragment of marble was found bearing a list of twenty-four families of priests who took turns in serving in the Jerusalem temple. It is the only inscription we possess which shows the name of Nazareth. One of the families in question must have lived there, probably driven out of the Holy City by the Romans. They would hardly have chosen Nazareth, unless others, who shared their spiritual belief, lived there.

Jesus received his early religious instruction at home. His father must have taught him the well-known *Sh'ma:* "Hear, O Israel: The Lord our God is one Lord; and you shall love the Lord your God with all your heart.... And these words which I command you this day shall be upon your heart; and you shall teach them diligently to your children..." (Deuteronomy 6:4–8).

Perhaps Jesus asked, "What is the meaning of the testimonies and the statutes and the ordinances which the Lord our God has commanded you?" And his father would have answered, "We were Pharaoh's slaves in Egypt; and the Lord brought us out of Egypt with a mighty hand.... And it will be righteousness for us, if we are careful to do all this commandment before the Lord our God, as he has commanded us" (Deuteronomy 6:20–25).

Individual life was governed by prayer: "The Holy One, let us praise him." Of special importance were the prayers said in the home. Before every meal, the father spoke a blessing over bread and wine and ended with a prayer of thanksgiving and praise. The great climax of the year was the Passover celebration. Theoretically, it should have been held in Jerusalem where the heads of families slaughtered lambs in the forecourt of the Temple and then brought the meat home to be cooked and eaten. Outside of Jerusalem, however, the Passover ceremony was shorter and did not include the killing of lambs. It was, primarily, a children's festival and they were entitled to ask questions about the meaning of the various rites. It was also a time when messianic hopes were expressed, and all those present prayed that the revered prophet Elijah might soon come bringing joyful tidings, help and comfort, and, finally, that the merciful God would grant them the advent of the Messiah.

Christian households assemble to read the Bible. Jewish families say many prayers together at home and this strengthens the faith and gives children a definite place in the whole community. There are also divine services in the synagogue where the ritual is confined to words: reading, chanting and preaching. The cantor intones the Sh'ma, a passage from the Torah, and the Prophets is read and expounded. The service ends with a blessing spoken by the priest. The synagogue is not only a place of devotion but a house for general assembly (Beit Knesset) where the faithful can meet and converse. Each synagogue faces Jerusalem, to symbolize the idea that all roads lead to the Holy City.

Special honor is conferred on the shrine that houses Torah scrolls, and also the lectern. Early in life, Jesus must have become familiar with the sacred texts of the scrolls and their Hebrew idiom. At that time, there were many synagogues in Galilee, the earliest one known dating from the third or fourth

Sinai oases are characteristically marked by date groves. Traveling to Egypt, Jesus and his parents must have partaken of such sweet dates.

century. The first pilgrims to Nazareth mention a synagogue which later became a church. Where this building stood we do not know for sure. Perhaps the remains of a synagogue found under the Basilica of the Annunciation are part of it.

Jesus' adult religious outlook was almost certainly influenced by his childhood experiences, and by the education he received as he grew up. His habit of deep prayer must have been prompted by the tradition of prayer in the home. Once, when a scribe asked him which was the most important commandment, he replied unhesitatingly with the *Sh'ma*. We know from the Gospels that he read Isaiah (51:1ff.) and expounded the meaning of the text.

BAR MITZVAH

Another important event in Jesus' childhood is also mentioned in the Gospels. Yearly, his parents made their pilgrimage to Jerusalem and, when Jesus was twelve years old, they took him along. There was no longer any personal danger for the family going south because Archelaus, whom they had purposely

Returning to Israel, the Holy Family bypassed Bethlehem and traveled to the north
and Galilee. Legend has it that, before
leaving the coast, they spent one night in a
cave at the foot of Mount Carmel.

avoided in Bethlehem, had been deposed and a Roman procurator, Coponius, was appointed for the first time. However, the main reason for Jesus' visit was that he was reaching his thirteenth birthday, when a young Jew becomes *Bar Mitzvah,* a son of commandment. From then on, as far as religion is concerned, he is treated as an adult. He is allowed to read from the Torah in the synagogue and to ask questions about it. The family journey was a true pilgrimage to the Jerusalem temple.

Pilgrimage is distinct from other travel in that it is undertaken only by someone who lives in a foreign place, in exile, and yearns for his true spiritual home. Jews believed that God's presence was especially close in the temple and their greatest wish was to be with him there (Psalm 27:4–5). The pilgrim needs the company of others who share his faith, to pray and sing together, and so prepare for the great event. Jewish pilgrimages were made in groups, consisting of families, kinsfolk and fellow villagers, all united with the hope of receiving God's blessing on their community.

We can imagine how overwhelmed the boy Jesus must have been at the first sight of the magnificent temple, *the* place of God's presence. In Solomon's Portico (the eastern portico was named after King Solomon), the young man became *Bar Mitzvah,* in a dialogue with the rabbis, whom he astounded with his questions and answers. He stayed on for several days after his parents had left for home and, when his worried mother finally found him, he said to her enigmatically, "Did you not know that I must be in my Father's house?" (Luke 2:49). This is one of Jesus' most original sayings. In it he speaks of God as his father for the first time, and so reveals the secret of his real origin.

Jesus' next years spent in Nazareth were unruffled by outside events. People in contact with him did not know who he really was, but his mother, Mary, stored up everything that happened in her heart. Jesus spent his time getting to know the world around him, watching the sower at his work and walking through the fields where the corn stood high. Sometimes, he would climb a vineyard watchtower during the vintage or linger with

shepherds as they tended their flocks. He
knew the secrets of the fig tree, the briar, the
sycamore and the tiny mustard seed which
grows into such a large bush. He knew the
ways of foxes and how birds built their nests.
All this was, for him, a manifestation of God's
own glory and he would later fill his preaching
with images drawn from nature.

Most of all, he observed people. For him,
they were children of God and he conversed
with them continually. The poor, the outcast,
the suffering, the mourners, strangers like the
Samaritans — all had a particular interest for
him. By Lake Kinnereth he would also meet
Greeks, for there were two Greek-speaking
towns, Hippos (near modern Ein Gev) and
Gadara (near Umm Qeis) by the edge of the
water. Living in a country that is really a
corridor, the inhabitants have always been
familiar with foreign languages. Today, every
Arab boy has a smattering of English and
Hebrew. People here have a good ear and a
retentive memory, making it easy for them to
pick up foreign words and phrases. In
everyday life, Jesus spoke Aramaic; his
prayers he said in Hebrew. Since, later, he

child grew and became strong, filled with wisdom" *(Luke 2:39–40)*

There were many house-caves in the mountainous areas of the Holy Land. Tradition has it that Jesus was reared in one (left), beneath the Church of St. Joseph. Three frescoes decorate the apses of St. Joseph's Church. One (right) depicts the Holy Family.

was able to speak with Pilate without an interpreter, we can assume that he also knew a certain amount of Greek.

Very little is known of his personal appearance. There is no contemporary representation, and in Byzantine mosaics he is pictured according to theological concepts of the time. His garments must have been the customary ones: a sleeveless gown covered by another, sandals and a staff. His head may have been protected by a white cloth, similar to the Arab kaffiyeh, held in place with a cord. Typical of the inhabitants of this land are large dark eyes, deep and compassionate, but quick to express fear in an unfamiliar situation. This characteristic of the eyes helps to explain why so much importance is given in the Bible to the act of looking. However, people are usually reserved and do not readily betray their feelings. Loud laughter is rarely heard, and there has never been any mention of Jesus laughing aloud. Looking at a trusting young man who queried him about eternal life, he may have allowed himself a smile (Mark 10:21). Sometimes, people weep in a quiet, reserved way, especially men, when

"And when he was twelve years old, they went up (to Jerusalem) according to custom" (Luke 2:42)

This is how the Jerusalem temple looked in Jesus' time, according to a reconstruction recently made in Jerusalem. Within, at the age of twelve, he gave proof of his knowledge of the Law to Jerusalem teachers.

they have sustained a great personal loss, such as a bereavement. Jesus wept for Lazarus when he died, and also wept for Jerusalem's future. However, people soon regain their self-control and only the sadness in their eyes reveals that they have been greatly grieved. Jesus' voice must have been fascinating to people and they "wondered at the gracious words which proceeded out of his mouth" (Luke 4:22). The same voice could be most effective, as, for example, when he called a dead man from the grave: "Lazarus, come out" (John 11:43).

We can only guess how much Jesus knew of world events and their effect on his immediate surroundings. People of Nazareth would have heard of the death of the former governor of Syria, Quintilius Varus, who sent the rebels of nearby Sepphoris into slavery, and had two thousand resistance fighters crucified. Emperor Augustus died when Jesus was twenty years old. It was the image of his successor, Tiberius, which was on the Roman denarius when Pharisees showed Jesus a coin of the realm, in connection with a discussion about taxes. New Roman procurators came to the Holy Land and Judea. The fifth in order of succession was Pontius Pilate (26–36/37 A.D.). He had his headquarters in Caesarea by the Sea, and recently his name has been found on a stone among the ruins of the Roman amphitheater of the town. Even before the time of Pilate, complications in matters of a religious nature had occurred because the procurators had begun to appoint and dismiss high priests, according to whim. Caiaphas, destined to conduct proceedings leading to Jesus' death, was promoted to the post when Jesus was twenty-five years old. The fact that the Gospel writers were thoroughly familiar with contemporary events is evidenced in Luke's calendar: "In the fifteenth year of the reign of Tiberius Caesar, Pontius Pilate being governor of Judea, and Herod being tetrarch of Galilee, and his brother Philip tetrarch of the region of Iturea and Trachonitis, and Lysanias tetrarch of Abilene, in the high-priesthood of Annas and Caiaphas..." (Luke 3:1–2).

CHAPTER 4 EMERGING

In which Jesus steps out of Nazareth into the world

About the beginning of 28 A.D., Jesus was seen on the lower reaches of the Jordan. He had left the quiet life of Nazareth and, as many others did, had come to see John the Baptist. "John the baptizer appeared in the wilderness, preaching a baptism of repentance for the forgiveness of sins. And there went out to him all the country of Judea, and all the people of Jerusalem; and they were baptized by him in the river Jordan, confessing their sins. Now John was clothed with camel's hair, and had a leather girdle around his waist, and ate locusts and wild honey."

John followed the tradition of ancient prophets, proclaiming a coming disaster by means of familiar references drawn from people's daily lives. God in his mercy had allowed the Chosen People certain privileges, but that should be no reason for individual complacency. On the contrary, it is necessary for each individual to repent and to acknowledge the living God here and now: "Bear fruit that befits repentance, and do not presume to say to yourselves, 'We have Abraham as our father'; for I tell you, God is able from these stones to raise up children to Abraham. Even now the axe is laid to the root of the trees; every tree therefore that does not bear good fruit is cut down and thrown into the fire" (Matthew 3:7–10).

BAPTISM

As the stranger, Jesus, approached, John exclaimed, "After me comes he who is mightier than I, the thong of whose sandals I am not worthy to stoop down and untie. I have baptized with water; but he will baptize you with the Holy Spirit" (Mark 1:7–8). John's baptism cleansed people and symbolized their change of heart, but baptism by the Messiah would infuse them with the spirit and newness of life. John was the first to see such an intervention on the part of God and, specifically, in relation to Jesus: "In those days Jesus came from Nazareth of Galilee and was baptized by John in the Jordan. And when he came up out of the water, immediately he saw the heavens opened and the Spirit descending upon him like a dove; and a voice from heaven, 'Thou art my beloved Son; with thee I am well pleased'" (Mark 1:9–11).

72

The background is the Jordan, a very special river, twisting and turning as it winds its way through the deepest valley on earth. Though sometimes flooded, the Jordan has had no economic significance through the ages. Easily forded, it hardly interferes with passing traffic. In the summertime, it can be crossed on foot. Yet, from the religious viewpoint, it is quite unique. As the well-known archaeologist, Nelson Glueck, has put it: "Its basic importance cannot be magnified, because its role in history has been beyond all rational measurement; it is in connection with the revelation of the divine that the importance of the Jordan River becomes paramount, exceeding that of any other river in the world."

Unlike many other holy rivers, its healing powers are not proclaimed. Its great importance lies in the fact that it is the natural boundary of the Promised Land. When Jacob crossed it, he was conscious of something decisive, since he was returning to the land promised the Patriarchs. Moses, at the climax of his career, was not allowed to go beyond it. Joshua crossed it in solemn pro-cession, leading his people into the land which God had promised. Great meaning is given this fording of the Jordan in the Book of Deuteronomy: "Hear, O Israel; you are to pass over the Jordan this day.... Know therefore this day that he who goes over before you... is the Lord your God" (9:1, 3).

Thus, the entry into the land of Canaan is indeed a "transition," not only in the literal but also in the religious sense. It proves that the people have been under God's guidance all along, and that they have now come into the inheritance designated by Him. Just so, the baptism of Jesus by John is also a turning point. The Holy Ghost had descended on Jesus and the voice of the Father had acknowledged him as his son. Jesus, another Joshua, is ready to begin his task of leading his people into the kingdom of God.

The site of the baptism was probably on the east bank of the river. According to the Gospel (John 1:28), John the Baptist was active in Bethany beyond the Jordan, and he may well have chosen the very ford which the Children of Israel had used as a crossing (Joshua 3:14–16). After the Arab conquest,

Just before flowing into the Dead Sea, the Jordan River makes the surrounding desert bloom. Here, John baptized Jesus.

Christian imagination transferred the site of the baptism to the west bank, and many chapels and monasteries of different denominations line it now. From very early times, pilgrims were accustomed to take home a little Jordan water for their relatives and friends. On the feast of the Epiphany, thousands of Greek Orthodox Christians come to the river to renew their baptism symbolically. Gathered on boats, Catholics chant passages from the Gospels telling of Christ's own baptism.

After being baptized by John, Jesus withdrew into the desert to pray and fast, according to the example set by John. It was during this time that the devil tempted Jesus (Luke 4:1–13). A tradition, which originated much later, has it that he sat on a mountain, contemplating the valley below and meditating. In reality, he must have moved about in the wilderness, crossing its barren ridges and deep gullies. The desert is a place of grace, revealing the magnitude and majesty of creation reflected in the landscape. However, it is also a place of temptation because of its desolation and loneliness.

It was natural that tradition should try to localize the place where Jesus experienced temptation. The apocryphal *Gospel according to the Hebrews* fixed it on Mount Tabor. Possibly the very landscape suggested the victory of Jesus over Satan. However, since Byzantine times, the sheer cliff face, west of Jericho's oldest area, has been venerated as the site. There, numerous grottos, both natural and man-made, soon began to attract hermits and monks. The most distinguished among them were St. Chariton and St. Elpidius, who wanted to live in places made holy by the Bible and according to the example of Christ. Halfway up the hillside, a Greek monastery still perches like an aerie. A cave within, now turned into a chapel, is said to have been one of the places where Jesus dwelt.

The Gospel story may create the impression that what John the Baptist was doing was quite extraordinary, even unique. Yet, we know that, in his time, there were many others who preached repentance. A great number of religiously minded people, longing for the coming of the Messiah, dwelt precisely in this

74

Galilee and was baptized by John in the Jordan'' (Mark 1:9)

same area of the Judean Desert near the Dead Sea. This has been emphasized again in our own time by the discovery of the ruins of a Jewish monastery at Qumran, together with priceless texts in nearby caves (1947).

THE WEDDING IN CANA

Soon after his baptism and the experience in the desert, Jesus returned to Galilee and, accompanied by his mother and some disciples whom he was attracting, he attended a farmer's wedding at Cana in Galilee. According to custom, such festivities began on the third day of the week and lasted about seven days. There was usually a risk of supplies running out, as they did on this occasion. But thanks to the intervention of his mother, Jesus came to the rescue in a remarkable way. "When the wine failed, the mother of Jesus said to him, 'They have no wine.' And Jesus said to her, 'O woman, what have you to do with me? My hour has not yet come.' His mother said to the servants, 'Do whatever he tells you.' Now six stone jars were standing there, for the Jewish rites of purification, each holding twenty or thirty gallons. Jesus said to them, 'Fill the jars with water.' And they filled them up to the brim. He said to them, 'Now draw some out, and take it to the steward of the feast.' So they took it. When the steward of the feast tasted the water now become wine, and did not know where it came from (though the servants who had drawn the water knew), the steward of the feast called the bridegroom and said to him, 'Every man serves the good wine first; and when men have drunk freely, then the poor wine; but you have kept the good wine until now.'" (John 2:3–10).

The evangelist then expressly adds: "This, the first of his signs, Jesus did at Cana in Galilee, and manifested his glory; and his disciples believed in him." This first show of Jesus' power involved a deep revelation. He was not an ascetic, living in solitude in the desert. He went among ordinary, simple folk, bringing them happiness. Still, we should not stop short of the actual miracle which helped poor people overcome temporary embarrassment, but try to fathom the profound, mysterious meaning of the story relative to Christ. As he will state plainly

"...he fasted forty days and forty nights, and afterward he was hungry" *(Matthew 4:2)*

Jesus fasted for forty days before beginning his public preaching. In the end, the devil sought to deflect him from his holy purpose. Legend has it that Jesus sat on this stool-shaped rock, resisting Satan's temptations. It is now kept in a monastery on the Hill of the Temptation, near Jericho.

later, he is the grapevine providing spiritual life for all men (John 15:1). The steward's comment to the bridegroom about keeping the best wine until last may sound like a joke but, in reality, it has very deep meaning. Therefore, here in Cana, Jesus demonstrated that he was very different from members of the Qumran community, and very different even from John. Here, at the very beginning of his public ministry, his disciples began to realize that he was unique.

About seven miles out of Nazareth, on the highway to the Sea of Galilee, the harp-shaped lake which is also called the Lake Kinnereth, Lake Gennesareth and Lake Tiberias, stands the Arab village of Cana, surrounded by pomegranate and olive groves and dominated by a Latin church with its red cupola and twin towers. In its crypt there are replicas of earthenware pots. The place must be very ancient, as is borne out by the remains of a synagogue discovered there. However, another place, close by, also claims to be the site of the first miracle. It also shows traces of early habitation but we must await fuller excavation before deciding defi-

"...Jesus was led up by the Spirit into the wilderness to be tempted by the devil"

(Matthew 4:1)

In early times, hermits built a cliff-hanging monastery on the Hill of the Temptation, marking Jesus' fast in this place. It is now known as the "Mount of Quarantine" (Forty).

nitely. However, these conflicting claims are of purely topographical interest. More important is the typically Oriental scene presented by modern Cana. The town which Jesus knew must have looked very much like it.

JERUSALEM

Soon after the marriage feast of Cana, Jesus went to Jerusalem for the festival of Passover and there, again, he attracted great attention. As with every Jew, a visit to Jerusalem must have stirred him deeply. Within ten miles from the city, he would have had his first glimpse of the capital. His heart must have throbbed with the emotion well expressed in an ancient poem:

"I was glad when they said to me,
    'Let us go to the house of the Lord!'
Our feet have been standing
    within your gates, O Jerusalem!
Jerusalem, built as a city
    which is bound firmly together,
To which the tribes go up,
    the tribes of the Lord,
As was decreed for Israel,

"... he came to Nazareth ... he went to the synagogue

The remains of an ancient synagogue in
Nazareth, said to have been Jesus'
school and the scene of his first preaching in Galilee. Once, when he applied
a passage from the book of Isaiah
to himself, the audience grew so angered
that his very life was endangered.

to give thanks to the name of the Lord.
There thrones for judgment were set,
  the thrones of the house of David.
Pray for the peace of Jerusalem!
  'May they prosper who love you!
Peace be within your walls
  and security within your towers!'
For my brethren and companions' sake
  I will say, 'Peace be within you!'
For the sake of the house of the Lord our God,
  I will seek your good."

(Psalm 122).

Characteristic of the Middle East is the
fact that certain places remain holy through
the centuries, even though another religion
may be practiced there. Today, the Moslem
Dome of the Rock in Jerusalem is a center of
attraction, just as the temple on the same site
once was. Visiting Jerusalem, Jesus would
have been impressed by the magnificent temple,
which had been recently rebuilt by Herod. It
spread over thirty-five acres, surrounded by
double colonnades. The Jewish historian
Josephus has left us the following description:
"All the cloisters were double, and the pillars
belonging to them were twenty-five cubits in
height, supporting the cloisters. These pillars
were of one entire stone each, and that stone
was white marble; and the roofs were
adorned with cedar, curiously graven. The
natural magnificence and excellent polish and
the harmony of the joints in these cloisters
afforded a prospect that was very remarkable;
nor was it adorned on the outside with any
work of the painter or engraver. The cloisters
(of the outmost court) were thirty cubits in
breadth, while the entire compass of it was
six furlongs in size, including the tower of
Antonia; those entire courts that were exposed
to the air were paved with all sorts of stones"
(Jewish War 5, 5, 2).

The eastern portico was named after
Solomon; the one to the south, dominating
the valley of Kidron, was called "Royal." On
the east side, the area was bounded by the
so-called pinnacle of the temple mentioned
in the story of Jesus' temptation (Matthew
4:5). There were eight gates leading into the
temple, including the double gate named
Hulda, which gave entry from the south and
passed underneath the Royal Porch. To the
east, was the Gate of Susa, still to be seen,

81

"And they... led him to the brow of the hill on which their city was built, that they might throw him down headlong" (Luke 4:29)

The Mount of the Precipitation. Legend has it that it was from this crag that Jesus' fellow-citizens sought to cast him down. Nowadays, it is believed that the incident occurred above Nazareth's own valley, within the town limits.

and called the Golden Gate. It was walled up by the Byzantines. The main gate, called the Gate of Coponius (after the first Roman procurator), was in the western wall. It was decorated with a golden eagle, a symbol that the whole temple had been placed under the protection of Rome. Anyone could enter the outer area which was, therefore, called the Court of the Gentiles.

The temple area proper was enclosed by a balustrade and, at the entrance, there were warning notices, one of which is still preserved in the Istanbul Museum. It states that foreigners have freedom of access provided they do not go beyond the balustrade. No uncircumcized person could cross it, under pain of death. Fourteen steps led through the Beautiful Gate to the Court of the Women. Therein were placed the poor boxes, one of which received the widow's mite — small contributions — mentioned in the Gospel (Luke 21:1–4). Another fifteen steps led up to the famous Gate of Nicanor where Mary brought her infant at the time of the Presentation. This led through the Court of the Men to that of the priests with the altar for burnt

offerings in the center and the large basin on the left, called the Brazen Sea, resting on twelve bulls cast in bronze.

Additional steps led up to the temple proper, a comparatively small structure, whose interior was concealed from view by a priceless curtain, embroidered with a map of the then-known world. Open only to the priest on duty, it housed the golden altar on which incense was offered and, next to it, the seven-branched candlestick. The table with the twelve loaves of shewbread (replaced each Sabbath) also stood there. Finally, still farther inside, there was the Holy of Holies which the high priest alone was permitted to enter, only on the Day of Atonement. A stone marked the spot where the Ark of the Covenant had once stood.

PRESERVING SANCTITY

Jesus must have been deeply impressed with the holiness of the temple and this explains his demonstration within its precints, remembered as long as he lived, as well as being the ultimate cause of his death. According to the chronology of the Fourth Gospel, this

> *"And he (Jesus) went about all Galilee, teaching in their synagogues and preaching the gospel of the kingdom..."*
>
> *(Matthew 4:23)*

The wooded hills of Galilee were the scene of much of Jesus' public ministry.

occurred on his first public visit to Jerusalem: "In the temple he found those who were selling oxen and sheep and pigeons, and the money changers at their business. And making a whip of cords, he drove them all, with the sheep and oxen, out of the temple; and he poured out the coins of the money changers and overturned their tables. And he told those who sold the pigeons, 'Take these things away; you shall not make my Father's house a house of trade'" (John 2:14–16).

As taxes for the temple were due at this time, the money changers had come into the forecourts together with those who sold animals for sacrifice. Jesus was intent on preserving the purity of the temple rites and his behavior was justified. Nevertheless, the event caused a great disturbance. The temple police appeared and questioned him: "What sign have you to show us for doing this?" (John 2:18).

Jesus answered them enigmatically: "Destroy this temple, and in three days I will raise it up" (John 2:19). His listeners naturally thought he was referring to the physical structure of the temple built with stone. Jesus,

however, was referring to his own body which would rise again after violent death. This is how the first public misunderstanding had occurred.

At that same time Jesus met Nicodemus, a Pharisee and a member of the Sanhedrin, the supreme council and tribunal of the Jews. Behind the encounter we can glimpse the diversity of religious parties of the era. Everyone shared the common hope of the imminent coming of the Messiah, but beliefs about it differed greatly. There were the Zealots, for instance, idealists who were, at the same time, intensely nationalistic. They believed that Jewish deliverance should be brought about by political revolt. Priests and lay aristocracy were members of the Sadducees. They held to the strict observance of the Law and rejected the so-called Traditions of the Fathers. Their theological teachings were quite definitive. They did not believe in the resurrection of the dead, the immortality of the soul and the concept of reward and punishment in a life hereafter. They were well known for their strict dealings in matters of justice, following the rule, "an eye for an

84

eye, and a tooth for a tooth." In Jesus' time they had lost much of their influence to the Pharisees.

The latter were the "separatists," rejecting all non-Jewish influences and, in particular, the Hellenistic. They strove to keep themselves pure and, because of this, tax collectors, open sinners, harlots and others could not join their sect. Their aim was that "the true Israel" should become manifest in daily life. Their supreme guiding principle was the Law, which always had to be interpreted according to changing economic and political conditions.

To bring this about, the help of the scribes was needed. These people attracted members of the petty bourgeoisie (tradesfolk, craftsmen, day laborers) and their influence stemmed from their minute knowledge of the Law. When the wise men from the East appeared at Herod's court asking where the new king of the Jews had been born, the scribes answered promptly by quoting from the prophet Micah (5:2). They were highly esteemed for the numerous years they had spent in study of the Law, and they were experts in the field of justice, as well as its disseminators and administrators. They bore the honorable title of rabbi. They tried to gear the Law to daily events in everyday life, providing innumerable rules of behavior in the form of strict commandments and prohibitions. In so doing, they developed a very subtle system of precepts. Believing that the Law could be observed quite literally, they rejected the judgment preached by the Baptist and the call of Jesus to repent.

Jesus' story of the Pharisee and the tax collector provides a good example of what the Pharisees stood for: "Two men went up into the temple to pray, one a Pharisee and the other a tax collector. The Pharisee stood and prayed thus with himself, 'God, I thank thee that I am not like other men, extortioners, unjust, adulterers, or even like this tax collector. I fast twice a week, I give tithes of all that I get.' But the tax collector, standing far off, would not even lift his eyes to heaven, but beat his breast, saying, 'God, be merciful to me, a sinner!' I tell you, this man went down to his house justified rather than the other."

The Pharisee was undoubtedly sincere in his own way. However, he confronted God

"Consider the lilies, how they grow; they neither toil nor spin" (Luke 12:27)

Springtime in the Holy Land brings a feast for the eye and joy for the soul. All Galilee is in bloom, and the Sea of Galilee forms a vision of blue. Jesus often illustrated his teachings by references to such wonders of nature.

with a personal theme with his repeated "I, I, I." The tax collector, on the other hand, said very little. He did not discuss facts but addressed God directly, intent on a dialogue with his Maker. The Pharisee's piety was hackneyed and impersonal. The tax collector had a living faith, seeking to enter into a close, personal relationship with God.

Monologue — dialogue; these are symptoms of the great differences which divided Jesus from the Pharisees. This is why Jesus fought against the strict observance of the Sabbath, the literal interpretation of laws on purification, fasting and praying. In the Gospels, the Pharisees are often portrayed as hypocrites, and the contrast between their theories and practices is criticized. However, this is frequently true of any religion, once its vital observance turns into a fixed formula. Not only Jewry, but all religious communities run this risk. All Pharisaic perplexity on problems presented to Jesus is symbolized in the conversation between him and Nicodemus. The latter just could not understand that one needs to be reborn (of "water and the Spirit") in order to see the kingdom of God.

88

CHAPTER 5 NORTHWARD AGAIN

In which Jesus begins his ministry

For some time after Passover, Jesus stayed on in Judaea where he had been baptized. Then he went back north. The reason for this was that he had come under suspicion on the part of the Pharisees, because he was attracting even more followers than John. Wishing to avoid an open conflict with the authorities, Jesus deemed it better to withdraw. Besides, news of the Baptist's arrest was broadcast. He had publicly accused Herod Antipas of adultery, and was made prisoner in the fortress of Machaerus, east of the Dead Sea.

SAMARIA

Jesus' journeys from Nazareth to Jerusalem and back led him through the hilly countryside of Samaria, past the ancient capital of the area Jeremiah called "Samaria's green garland." It had been restored to its former beauty by Herod, who named it Sebastos in honor of the emperor Augustus. The road ran through the ancient town of Sichem, lying in a valley between Mount Ebal and Mount Garizim. Here Samaritans sometimes showed hostility to Jews by refusing them hospitality. The differences between the two peoples arose from the fact that the Samaritans were a mixed race, the product of unions between Jews and settlers from abroad, who came into the region after the Assyrian conquest in 722 B.C. When the Jews returned from exile (from 537 B.C. onward) they spurned the help of the Samaritans in rebuilding the temple in Jerusalem. The Samaritans, therefore, built their own shrine on Mount Garizim and brought animals there to be sacrificed in accordance with the local tradition. From the theological point of view, Samaritanism was basically a sect within Judaism, having affinities with the Sadducees as well as with the kind of people that formed the Qumran community. There were age-old tensions between north and south — Samaria and Jerusalem — and these are reflected quite clearly in the Bible. The beginnings of Samaritanism as a separate entity, typical of an isolated, mountainous region, can be dated back to the third or second century B.C.

In modern times, about three hundred Samaritans still live in the district and celebrate Passover each year, according to their own interpretation of the Torah. It was here that Jesus faced the problem not only of where God should be worshiped (Zion or Garizim) but also of the very human hostility of one community against another, since Jews heartily despised Samaritans. That the problem disturbed Jesus is evident from his parable of the Good Samaritan (Luke 10:29–37), especially from the story of his meeting with the Samaritan woman and her people (John 4:7–26). Starting with his request for a drink of well water, it leads on to an explanation of his claim to plant within the human personality "a spring of water welling up to eternal life" (John 4:6–26). The background of the conversation was Jacob's Well — a stopover place for caravans since ancient times — perpetuating the memory of the Patriarch who first dug the well in an open field. Its great depth can still be tested. At approximately 105 feet below there is fresh underground water. Early in the Christian story, it became a shrine, and St. Jerome tells us that a church had been built there by his time. The Crusaders erected a basilica with three naves on the spot, and two flights of stairs led down to the crypt housing the brim of the well. This remained after the man-made structures above ground fell into ruin, in the course of time. Before the First World War, plans were made to build a new church on that site but, due to the war, work stopped and, today, only the incomplete outer walls stand.

BY THE SEA OF GALILEE

Jesus then began his public ministry in Galilee. Mark, relying on Peter's word, sums it up: "The time is fulfilled, and the kingdom of God is at hand; repent, and believe in the gospel" (Mark 1:15). With Jesus' inauguration of the kingdom of God, the time decided on by Providence had been fulfilled. For mankind, this was the hour of decision, calling for conversion, change of mind and heart, then faith in Jesus Christ. His public ministry evolved around the Sea of Galilee. The Jordan passes through the lake which lies about seven hundred feet below sea level. The surrounding landscape is quite unique. On the east and west, the terrain rises to a fertile plateau. From above, the water appears to be a very deep blue. From the southern shore, the twin peaks of Mount

Cana lies in a small valley north-east of Nazareth and has preserved its Oriental character. Jesus and Mary were guests at a wedding feast in the hamlet.

Canaan are visible, as well as the mountain town of Safed, whose bright lights at night recall Jesus' reference to a city which can never be hid (Matthew 5:14). In the distance, snow-covered Mount Hermon rises. With its multihued appearance, it seems to belong to another world. On the eastern shore gleam the small white homes of Ein Gev. Immediately behind the kibbutz is the steep hill on which Hellenistic Hippos stood. On the northwestern shore, there is the charming Bay of Magdala. Between the ruins of Tabgha and Capernaum, groves of willow and eucalyptus form oases. The first impression of solitude and desolation is misleading, as in ancient times the whole district was one vast orchard and this is slowly being restored today by intense cultivation in the new settlements.

Josephus gives a description of the earlier lushness. "The country that lies over against the lake had the same name of Gennesareth; its nature is wonderful as well as its beauty; its soil is so fruitful that all sorts of trees can grow upon it, and the inhabitants accordingly plant all kinds of trees there. For the temper of the air is so well mixed that it agrees well with those several varieties, particularly walnuts, which require the coldest air. There are palm trees also which grow best in hot air. Fig trees, also, and olives grow near them, requiring an air that is more temperate still. One may style this place nature's ambition where it forces those plants which are naturally mutual enemies to live in harmony. It is a happy striving of the seasons as if each laid claim to this country, for it not only nourishes various kinds of autumnal fruit, beyond human expectation, but preserves them a long time. It supplies men with the main fruits, with grapes and figs constantly through ten months of the year, and with the other fruits as they mature through the whole year. For, besides the fine temperate climate, it is also watered from a most abundant spring" *(Jewish War,* 3, 10, 8).

The Talmud says that the fruit of the district ripens faster than a deer can run, and that one can eat a hundred pieces and still want more. The fruit is so sweet that it has to be followed by something spicy, taken perhaps with bread.

94

The black basalt boulders covering the hill-sides are typical of the landscape, which was once volcanic. They are still used as masonry, and houses give the impression of something dark and sinister. This is true of the Roman theater in Gadara above lake level to the south. It is even truer of the ruins of Chorazin's synagogue above Capernaum. They stand blackly in sharp contrast to the glistening sunlight as if in answer to Jesus' words, "Woe to you, Chorazin!... for if the mighty works done in you had been done in Tyre and Sidon, they would have repented long ago in sackcloth and ashes" (Matthew 11:21).

The lake is usually calm. However, sudden storms can turn it into a raging sea. The lake is extraordinarily rich in fish and perhaps the best known is St. Peter's fish. The males of the species carry the eggs and the young in their mouths. The name was given because tradition has it that, at Jesus' command, a coin was to be found by Peter in the mouth of such a fish (Matthew 17:27). Nowadays, many fishing vessels exploit the lake and they are especially picturesque at night, as they float in line, with large lights aglow in each stern. During the day, fishermen can be seen mending their nets on the shore. It is easy to imagine Jesus crossing by boat from one side of the lake to the other.

In Jesus' time, there were a great number of towns and villages on the lake shore, especially on the western side. Tiberias, today the most important town of the area, is mentioned only in passing in the Gospels. Founded near hot springs, it was named by Herod Antipas after the Roman emperor of the time. Hot baths for medicinal purposes are now housed in a modern establishment, but they date back into antiquity. However, part of the old town was built over a cemetery and was, therefore, considered unclean and avoided by orthodox Jews. It achieved importance only after Jerusalem had been destroyed. This explains why it played no part in the story of Jesus.

Less than four miles to the north lies Magdala. This was the native town of Mary Magdalene, the first person to whom Jesus appeared after his resurrection (John 20:11). Prior to the prominence of Tiberias, Magdala was the chief settlement on the lake shore.

"On the third day there was a marriage at Cana in Galilee, and the mother of Jesus was there; Jesus also was invited to the marriage with his disciples" *(John 2:1–2)*

The Latin Church, Cana (left), modeled after the cathedral in Salzburg, Austria, commemorates Jesus' first miracle when he turned water into wine. A pitcher (right) recalls the first miracle.

"Jesus said to them, 'Fill the jars with water'" *(John 2:7)*

"As he walked by the Sea of Galilee, he saw two brothers, Simon who is called Peter and Andrew his brother, casting a net into the sea..." (Matthew 4:18)

Most of Jesus' public life was spent in the neighborhood of the Sea of Galilee (left). It is also known as Lake Tiberias, Lake Kinnereth and Lake Gennesareth. Many residents of the area gain a livelihood from fishing (below) in this wellstocked lake. Jesus' audiences often included fishermen of the region.

Josephus, however, must be exaggerating when he cites 40,000 as the number of its citizens. Its most important sources of income were weaving and fishing. Magdala salted fish were in demand from far-distant places. The ancient city possessed a hippodrome and this implies that at least part of its population must have been non-Jewish, possibly Hellenistic. Originally, the town stood right on the water's edge but silting caused it to move inland. Today, nothing remains as a clue to its former importance. Only excavations could throw light on its famous past. Farther to the north, the hills recede from the lakeside, giving way to the fertile plain of Gennesareth which, in turn, has given the lake another name.

From Magdala, Jesus often went to Bethsaida, east of where the Jordan entered the lake. This was once a big bay, but it has been filled with sand through the centuries. Large lagoons still remain, as reminders of this ancient feature. Bethsaida was the capital of the tetrarch Philip, who built it a couple of miles inland from the water's edge. The town was a center of a fishing industry and, according to the Talmud, three hundred different kinds of fish could be served in one dish. On the marshy ground near the Jordan, moorhens were caught and cooked as a favorite delicacy. This was a wealthy region, and a man like Zebedee must have had a thriving business employing many day laborers (Mark 1:19). Such economic prosperity was evidently detrimental to religious life there, for Jesus proclaimed, "Woe to you, Chorazin! Woe to you, Bethsaida!" (Matthew 11:21). Nevertheless, the most important personalities of the band of the apostles came from just this secularized area: Simon Peter, Andrew, Philip and Zebedee's sons, James and John.

CAPERNAUM

For headquarters, Jesus chose Capernaum (Kfar Nahum). He probably lived in the house of Simon Peter, making it his second home and the center of his ministry. Here, in "his" town, he preached more often and performed more miracles than anywhere else. The question naturally arises, why did Jesus settle precisely here? It is likely that the location of the town was an important factor in the decision. It was on the borders of the territories of Herod Antipas and Philip. It had a customhouse and a garrison under a centurion — a Roman captain. The customhouse supervised traffic on the lake. The inhabitants were industrious folk, judging from many basalt millstones and olive presses which have come to light. Here Jesus met the most diverse types of people and his message received a far greater response than it would ever have found in Nazareth.

Several decisive events in Jesus' life took place in Capernaum. He cured Peter's mother-in-law from fever (Matthew 8:14). At the request of the Roman centurion, he healed the officer's servant (Matthew 8:5–13). He restored to life the dead daughter of Jairus, the president of the synagogue, and he healed a cripple.

The last episode is typical of his ministry: "And when he returned to Capernaum after some days, it was reported that he was home. And many gathered together, so that there was no longer room for them, not even about the door; and he was preaching the word to them. And they came, bringing to him a paralytic carried by four men. And when they could not get near him because of the crowd, they removed the roof above him; and when they had made an opening, they let down the pallet on which the paralytic lay. And when Jesus saw their faith, he said to the paralytic, 'My son, your sins are forgiven.' Now some of the scribes were sitting there, questioning in their hearts, 'Why does this man speak thus? It is blasphemy! Who can forgive sins but God alone?' And immediately Jesus, perceiving in his spirit that they thus questioned within themselves, said to them, 'Why do you question thus in your hearts? Which is easier, to say to the paralytic, "Your sins are forgiven?" or to say, "Rise, take up your pallet and walk?" But that you may know that the Son of man has authority on earth to forgive sins' — he said to the paralytic — 'I say to you, rise, take up your pallet and go home.' And he rose, and immediately took up the pallet and went out before them all; so that they were all amazed and glorified God, saying, 'We never saw anything like this'" (Mark 2:1–12).

"And they went into Capernaum; and immediate

Jesus often preached in the synagogue of Capernaum, his second home. In the town he performed cures for the benefit of many, including, among others, the mother-in-law of Peter and the servant of the Roman centurion.

The story is told very graphically. Jesus returns quietly to Capernaum, but immediately the news spreads that he is home, probably at the house of Peter. Such a crowd collects that the stretcher bearers, wanting to bring the cripple in front of Jesus cannot force their way through. Without more ado, they climb the outside staircase leading to the roof, make an opening in the mud and straw covering, and lower the sick man until he rests directly in front of Jesus. This extraordinary procedure, disregarding all the generally accepted rules, shows how much confidence Jesus had already inspired. However, he does not wish to perform just another miracle and, therefore, speaks first about the remission of sins. This at once leads to an argument with the scribes who have come as passive, but critical observers. For them, Jesus' saying violates the divine order of things, as the remission of sins is only God's prerogative. To prove that his authority really comes from God, Jesus speaks the words which bring cure to the sick man. The result immediately imposes silence on the critics, but it also heightens the already exist-ing tension between Jesus and his enemies.

This passage (from Mark) also illustrates the vital nature of religious life in Capernaum, centered on the synagogue where Jesus delivered his sermons. One of the most important of these dealt with the bread of life: "I am the bread of life; he who comes to me shall not hunger, and he who believes in me shall never thirst" (John 6:35). From the bread that satisfies physical hunger he turns his attention to a different kind of bread, which he himself will provide.

In the course of the centuries, the town became covered with soil. However, two sacred buildings remained visible and, especially during the last fifty years, attracted the attention of archaeologists. Partially restored is the magnificent synagogue, once reached by a flight of imposing steps and containing three naves. It is especially noteworthy because of its symbolic ornamentation: palm trees, foliage, fruit, geometrical designs and a sculptured image of the Ark of the Covenant. It was built about 300 A.D. but almost certainly replaces an older synagogue, in which Jesus often preached.

n the sabbath he entered the synagogue and taught'' *(Mark 1:21)*

Capernaum's synagogue was beautifully decorated with carvings of traditional Jewish religious symbols including palm branches, pomegranates and citrons *(ethrog)*. The palm tree (right), symbolic of fertility in the Middle East, was commonly represented in early churches and synagogues, as here at Capernaum.

Not far from the synagogue is a Byzantine basilica with a baptistry. The floor of the church was once adorned by a magnificent mosaic representing a peacock, the whole body encircled by the colorful spread of the tail. Excavations beneath it (in 1968) found dwellings which must have belonged to the poorer people. However, one of these homes had been converted into a place of worship and, exactly above it, the Byzantine church was erected. Graffiti in Hebrew, Greek and Syriac, expressing prayerful invocations, indicate that the place of assembly underneath was frequented long before Byzantine times, and they bear out reports by pilgrims that the house of Simon Peter still stood in early Christian times, but was turned into a house of worship. Thus, Aetheria, a woman pilgrim from Spain, says, "The house of the prince of the apostles has been converted into a church, the walls of which are still standing."

There is no other place on earth where the proximity of a synagogue and a church is of such profound religious significance as in Capernaum. There are places which God seems to have chosen especially for his

revelation, such as mountains, hills and lakes. It is no accident that there is a synagogue near Lake Kinnereth together with the remains of Jesus' second home, later turned into a church.

THE APOSTLES ARE CHOSEN

At this time, when the crowds were milling around Jesus, there occurred the important event of the choice of the apostles. For this Jesus prepared in prayer to God. "And then he appointed the twelve, to be with him, and to be sent out to preach and have authority to cast out demons: Simon, whom he surnamed Peter; James the son of Zebedee and John the brother of James, both of whom he surnamed Boanerges, that is, sons of thunder; Andrew, and Philip, and Bartholomew, and Matthew, and Thomas, and James the son of Alphaeus, and Thaddaeus, and Simon the Cananaean, and Judas Iscariot, who betrayed him" (Mark 3:14–19).

The idea of the apostles is connected with the mission of the prophets, as written in Isaiah: "The Spirit of the Lord God is upon me, because the Lord has anointed me to

"he went up on the mountain ...and taught them, saying: 'Blessed are the poor in spirit'" (Matthew 5:1–3)

On a high hill north of the Sea of Galilee, Jesus preached the Sermon on the Mount. In commemoration, the Church of the Beatitudes was later built on the site. It overlooks the blue sea and the countryside sanctified by Jesus' words.

bring good tidings to the afflicted; he has sent me to bind up the brokenhearted, to proclaim liberty to the captives, and the opening of the prison to those who are bound" (61:1).

Now, however, the term "apostle" is interpreted in a special, Christian sense, inasmuch as the apostles are the legal, personal representatives of Jesus: "He who receives you receives me, and he who receives me receives him who sent me" (Matthew 10:140).

The number twelve corresponds to the twelve tribes of Israel. They will bear witness to the transition from the old Israel to the new. The apostles are Jesus' constant companions, and he initiates them into his secrets. Most important of all, they bear witness to his death and resurrection, wherein lies the root of Christian faith. Peter takes first place because he is destined to found the church. Judas, who will betray Jesus, comes last. With his origins in Judea, he is the only one who is not a Galilean. All these men were simple folk, neither Pharisees, scribes nor intellectuals. Jesus does not recognize social or cultural barriers; his only concern is

107

"He (Jesus)... taking the five loaves and the two fish h
gave the loaves to the disciples, and the disciples gave them t

ooked up to heaven,...
he crowds" (Matthew 14:19)

Two fishes and a basket of bread symbolize the miracle of the Multiplication of the loaves and fishes. The miracle took place, tradition says, at Tabgha (short for "Heptapegon," Greek for "Seven Springs"). The mosaic dates from the sixth century. Another detail from the mosaic floor (right): a peacock, symbolic of the immortality guaranteed by Christ.

that people be receptive to the word of God.

THE SERMON ON THE MOUNT

Everywhere in the villages and towns, Jesus preached the new righteousness based largely on the traditional concept of justice, which nevertheless acquires a new dimension by reason of his commandment that we must love even our enemies. On a mountainside, not far from Capernaum, crowded with people, Jesus solemnly pronounces the Beatitudes:

"Blessed are the poor in spirit, for theirs is the kingdom of heaven.

"Blessed are those who mourn, for they shall be comforted.

"Blessed are the meek, for they shall inherit the earth.

"Blessed are those who hunger and thirst for righteousness, for they shall be satisfied.

"Blessed are the merciful, for they shall obtain mercy.

"Blessed are the pure in heart, for they shall see God.

"Blessed are the peacemakers, for they

109

" …the kingdom of heaven is like a net which was thrown into the sea and gathered fish of every kind" (*Matthew 13:47*)

The so-called St. Peter's fish (*musht*) is the tastiest to be found in the Holy Land. In the miracle of the Multiplication, Jesus fed a large crowd with five loaves and two such fishes.

shall be called sons of God.

"Blessed are those who are persecuted for righteousness, for theirs is the kingdom of heaven.

"Blessed are you when men revile you and persecute you and utter all kinds of evil against you falsely on my account.

"Rejoice and be glad, for your reward is great in heaven, for so men persecuted the prophets who were before you."

(Matthew 5:3–12)

With the proclamation of the Beatitudes, the new order has been established. Now the kingdom of God alone means salvation; before it all worldly values are meaningless. As security for this new order stands Jesus who has spoken these words. The originality of Jesus centers precisely here, in his presentation of himself as decisive. Various attempts have been made to explain Christianity as arising from its immediate background, and the most recent suggestion would associate Jesus' person and teaching with a particular Jewish sect of his time now known to us from the discoveries at Qumran (since 1947). There are clear likenesses but also profound dif-

This small church (left), not far from the
Sea of Galilee, is in Migdal, ancient Magdala.
This was the home of Mary Magdalene who had
the courage to confess her sins and follow Jesus.
Wheat harvesting in Galilee (right). Passing
by such a wheat field on the sabbath, Jesus
permitted his disciples to pick a few ears and to
eat the grains. Thus, by his own
authority, Jesus broadened the narrow
interpretation of biblical laws.

ferences, as even a cursory examination will show.

The sect at Qumran said in prayer: "The abundance of his mercies toward all the sons of his grace" (Hymn 4:33).

Only a few miles away, the fields of Bethlehem heard the song on the first Christmas night: "Glory to God in the highest, and on earth peace among men with whom he is well pleased."

Qumran looks back to the covenant God made with his people. Bethlehem looks to the present time in which the Word dwells among us.

The teachings of Jesus center on the love we should show our fellow men: "But I say to you, Love your enemies and pray for those who persecute you" (Matthew 5:44). However, a Qumran teaching ran: "That they may love all that he has chosen and hate all that he has rejected" (Community Rule 1:4).

In Qumran, a strict line of division was drawn between the Chosen People and others: "And no man smitten with any human uncleanness shall enter the assembly of God; no man smitten in his flesh or

"...Jesus went through the grainfields on the sabbath; his disciples were hungry, and they began to pluck ears of grain and to eat" *(Matthew 12:1)*

In his travels, Jesus reached as far north as Caesarea Philippi, an area of lush vegetation where one of the sources of the Jordan flows (left). Niches cut in the rock (right) once housed idols of the Greek god Pan, whence the modern place name Baniyas. Here, Peter acknowledged Jesus as the Messiah. In return, Jesus told him, "You are Peter, the rock, and on this rock I will build my church."

"When Jesus came into the district of Caesarea Philippi, he asked his disciples, 'Who do men say that the Son of man is?" *(Matthew 16:13)*

Snow-capped Mount Hermon in the north of the
Holy Land seems to belong to another world.
It has been suggested that Hermon's peak
was the site of Jesus' Transfiguration.

paralyzed in his feet or hands or lame or
blind or deaf or dumb or smitten in his
flesh with a visible blemish; no old and
tottery man unable to stand still in the midst
of the congregation; none of these shall come
to hold office among the congregation of the
man" (Messianic Rule 2:5). Jesus, on the
other hand, gave these directions: "Go out
quickly to the streets and lanes of the city,
and bring in the poor and maimed and blind
and lame" (Luke 14:21).

In Qumran, much importance was attached
to the order of precedence: "Each man shall
sit in his place: the priests shall sit first and
the elders second, and all the rest of the people
according to their rank" (Community Rule
6:8). In the so-called Chapter Hall, the place
reserved for those higher in rank is marked
with a circle of stones still to be seen today.
Jesus, however, instructed his people: "So
the last will be first and the first last" (Matthew 20:16).

One of Jesus' deepest interests was mis-
sionary: "Go therefore and make disciples of
all nations, baptizing them in the name of the
Father and of the Son and of the Holy

"'Woe to you, Chorazin! woe to you, Bethsaida! for if the mighty works done in you had been done in Tyre and Sidon, they would have repented long ago in sackcloth and ashes'" (Matthew 11:21)

Some towns near the lakeshore of Galilee, like Chorazin and Bethsaida, refused to accept the teachings of Jesus and he cursed them.
The former site of Bethsaida (left). Ruins of the ancient synagogue of Chorazin (below).

Spirit" (Matthew 28:19). The sect of Qumran, on the contrary, rejected all contact with the rest of the world. The newcomer who wished to become a member of the community was commanded not to enter into conversation with those who were corrupt and to withhold from them the teaching of the commandments.

Many important sayings of Jesus have no counterpart whatsoever in Qumran: "And he who does not take his cross and follow me is not worthy of me" (Matthew 10:38). "I am the resurrection and the life; he who believes in me, though he die, yet shall he live" (John 11:25).

Many similarities can be explained by the common Jewish origin of both teachings. The differences were created by the person of Jesus, his crucifixion and his resurrection. In Qumran, everything centered on the observance and interpretation of the Torah. With Jesus, the focal point is his own personality, to which all precepts and foregoing examples must surrender their absolute value. Thus, he could say: "So it is lawful to do good on the sabbath" (Matthew 12:12).

It is likely that Jesus knew the community

"...Jesus took with him Peter and James and John his brother, and led them up a high mountain apart"

(Matthew 17:1)

According to Byzantine tradition, Mount Tabor
was the scene of Jesus' Transfiguration.
In the description of the event in the
New Testament, the mountain is not named.

at Qumran, at least from hearsay. It is not probable that he had anything to do with it, as its teachings do not basically agree with his own. John the Baptist is a little closer in spirit to Qumran, and he may even have belonged to it, for a time, in his youth. But, he, too, cut himself off from it, since he was concerned with the public preaching of penance and the conversion of people, while members of the Qumran sect had withdrawn from the world, shunning open activity.

Jesus and Qumran — chance or design? This question serves to emphasize the larger problem of the coexistence of Judaism and Christianity. At the same time, it is a reminder that there were, in Jesus' time, Jewish people of profound faith who sought solitude in the desert for contemplation, and whose way of life preceded Christian solitaries in the Judaean wilderness.

Where and exactly how Jesus spoke the Sermon on the Mount is of no great importance, since many hillsides by the lake must have echoed his voice as he preached one or another keynote of his teaching. However, at the beginning of the fifth century, Aetheria mentions a church built in commemoration of Jesus' sermon on the Beatitudes. Ruins of this church have been discovered near Tabgha Bay, and this must have been a site he frequented often. Recent archaeological explorations (1968) show that the locality was uninhabited until Byzantine times, so that, in Jesus' time, it was an open rocky area where people could gather without doing damage to cultivated fields. The modern Church of the Beatitudes, crowned with a cupola, stands farther up the hill and the view of the lake through its picture windows is extraordinarily beautiful. The panorama sweeps from the synagogue at Capernaum, visible through the trees, to the houses covering the Tiberias hills. This is the world in which Jesus preached to crowds and performed many miracles. Even if much of the detail is gone, the landscape remains forever, reflecting the glory of God. Even more important are his striking words depicted on the walls of the Church of the Beatitudes and engraved on the minds of millions who have accepted them as true.

CHAPTER 6 TEACHINGS AND ACCOMPLISHMENTS

In which Jesus makes his voice heard and begins to
worry the establishment

The wonders of nature, especially as manifested around the lake shore, impressed Jesus deeply. For him, God was scarcely hidden behind a screen of the unknown, since the supernatural world was symbolized by the marvels of what was natural. Therefore, Jesus' teaching was not delivered in abstract terms of philosophy or mysticism. It was constantly conveyed through references to everyday life: sowing, reaping, threshing, fishing, trading, patching, cooking and sweeping. Such a method of instruction was well known from the Old Testament. It was a comparison (parable, in the strict sense) but, more than that, it involved a challenge, piquing the curiosity of the listeners, making them reflect and urging them to evolve practical solutions in the deeper spheres of thought and life, especially in the realm of religion.

Jesus' approach may be summed up in his references to three staples of livelihood by the lake shore, the first one being grain. The basic belief of Christianity, in the death and resurrection of Jesus, was symbolized as follows: we have to believe in something that

dies before it produces new and abundant life. "Truly, truly, I say to you, unless a grain of wheat falls into the earth and dies, it remains alone; but if it dies it bears much fruit" (John 12:24).

The dynamics of the kingdom preached by Jesus was similarly brought home. It does not involve a sudden, dramatic inauguration of a new order, such as was hoped for by many contemporaries. On the contrary, the process is gradual and organic, but just as real as the development of a seed: "The kingdom of God is as if a man should scatter seed upon the ground, and should sleep and rise night and day, and the seed should sprout and grow, and he knows not how. The earth produces of itself, first the blade, then the ear, then the full grain in the ear" (Mark 4:26–28).

The kingdom preached by Christ does not transform men unnaturally or against their will. The spiritual fruit each one produces is in keeping with his own personality, his own response and his own free will. The diversity is comparable to the uneven harvests of Galilee: "A sower went out to sow. And as

On the main altar in the upper Church of the Transfiguration, six candlesticks stand in line with the crucifix.

he sowed, some seeds fell along the path, and the birds came and devoured them. Other seeds fell on rocky ground, where they had not much soil, and immediately they sprang up, since they had no depth of soil, but when the sun rose they were scorched; and since they had no root they withered away. Other seeds fell upon thorns, and the thorns grew up and choked them. Other seeds fell on good soil and brought forth grain, some a hundredfold, some sixty, some thirty" (Matthew 13:3–9).

PARABLES

Jesus was conscious that his method of preaching the Gospel, personally or through the apostles, could seem trivial in the eyes of those who awaited a spectacular inauguration of the messianic era. Yet, he assured his listeners that in time such modest beginnings would produce tremendous results, again like the small beginnings seen in nature itself: "With what can we compare the kingdom of God, or what parable shall we use for it? It is like a grain of mustard seed which, when sown upon the ground, is the smallest of all the

123

"...he was transfigured... his face shone like the sun, and his garments became white as light" (Matthew 17:2)

The peak of Tabor has been revered for thousands of years. Beyond the latticed gateway can be seen the Syrian-style Latin Church of the Transfiguration erected in 1924 on ancient foundations. In the translucent mosaic (right), Jesus is shown transfigured, flanked by Moses and Elijah. His face became radiant and his garments turned white as snow.

seeds on earth; yet when it is sown it grows up and becomes the greatest of all shrubs, and puts forth large branches, so that the birds of the air can make nests in its shade" (Mark 4:30–32).

The final outcome of the movement started by Jesus is similarly pictured. There were various individual responses, but in the end there would be a judgment, itself implying that free will has been respected. Therefore, during lifetimes and through history, good and bad are left to coexist, exactly as is seen in nature: "The kingdom of heaven may be compared to a man who sowed good seed in his field; but while men were sleeping, his enemy came and sowed weeds among the wheat, and went away. So when the plants came up and bore grain, then the weeds appeared also. And the servants of the householder came and said to him, 'Sir, did you not sow good seed in your field? How then has it weeds?' He said to them, 'An enemy has done this.' The servants said to him, 'Then do you want us to go and gather them?' But he said, 'No; lest in gathering the weeds you root up the wheat along with them.

Let both grow together until the harvest; and at harvest time, I will tell the reapers, Gather the weeds first and bind them in bundles to be burned, but gather the wheat into my barn,'" (Matthew 13:24–30).

One plant especially chosen for parabolic use by Jesus was the vine, which was so abundant in Galilee before the Arab occupation and the prohibition of wine. The gentle lake shore slopes are again covered by vineyards. Grapes are a choice growth and can symbolize spiritual refinement to be found only in men of good will: "You will know them by their fruits. Are grapes gathered from thorns, or figs from thistles? So, every sound tree bears good fruit, but the bad tree bears evil fruit. A sound tree cannot bear evil fruit, nor can a bad tree bear good fruit" (Matthew 7:16–18).

A good vintage results, not only from good vine stock, but from careful cultivation, especially pruning. So, the growth of the Christian movement through the world is based on the fact that Jesus, rooted in God, is the source of grace and men must draw their strength from him. Otherwise, they will be lopped off and discarded: "I am the vine and my Father is the vine-dresser. Every branch of mine that bears no fruit, he takes away, and every branch that does bear fruit, he prunes, that it may bear more fruit.... He who abides in me, and I in him, he it is that bears much fruit, for apart from me you can do nothing. If a man does not abide in me, he is cast forth as a branch and withers; and the branches are gathered, thrown into the fire and burned" (John 15:1–6). St. Augustine has the terse comment: *aut vitis aut ignis* (either the vine or the fire, of gehenna).

The novelty and richness of Jesus' teaching is such that it calls for new audiences, people not fixed in traditional prejudices or in slovenly ways of life. For this idea, too, he found an example in the new vintage process: "And no one puts new wine into old wineskins; if he does, the new wine will burst the skins and it will be spilled, and the skins will be destroyed. But new wine must be put into fresh wineskins" (Luke 5:37–38).

At Cana, Jesus enacted a parable by the deed of turning water into wine, bypassing the ordinary process of fermentation and maturing. This was something extraordinary, as is expressly noted in the narrative (John 2:1–11). Normally, Jesus stimulated people's minds and hearts as gently as nature itself.

Finally, the theme of shepherds and shepherding occurs in some of Jesus' most intimate expressions of love for his followers and for all men. In fact, the inner nature of the kingdom he founded is nowhere more clearly illustrated than by parable-allegories drawn from the ways of shepherds, so familiar to people of the Middle East both in antiquity and in our own times. Jesus says simply: "I am the good shepherd. The good shepherd lays down his life for the sheep.... I know mine and mine know me... and I lay down my life for my sheep" (John 10:11–14).

Through this imagery, Jesus claims to fulfill in detail all the work of guardianship and security which a true shepherd provides for his flock. "Truly, truly, I say to you, he who does not enter the sheepfold by the door but climbs in by another way, that man is a thief and a robber; but he who enters by the door is the shepherd of the sheep. To him the doorkeeper opens; the sheep hear

"*Jacob's well was there, and so Jesus, wearied as he was with his journey, sat down beside the well*" (*John 4:6*)

Returning to Galilee from Jerusalem, Jesus stopped in Samaria at Jacob's well (left). There he asked a woman for a drink and referred to himself as the source of water valid for eternal life. Samaritans in their annual Passover ceremony perform rites exactly as practiced in the time of Jesus. The tiny sect has preserved its own way of life around Mount Gerizim for some two thousand five hundred years.

"As he drew near to Jericho, a blind man was sitting by the roadside begging... And he cried, 'Jesus, Son of David, have mercy on me!'" (Luke 18:35; 38)

his voice, and he calls his own sheep by name and leads them out" (John 10:1–5). On another occasion, he warned against false teachers, again in terms of ravagers of the flock: "Beware of false prophets, who come to you in sheep's clothing, but inwardly are ravenous wolves" (Matthew 7:15).

Recalling many similar images in the Old Testament, Jesus describes God's love in terms of a shepherd who is dedicated to his flock almost to the point of folly: "What man of you, having a hundred sheep, if he has lost one of them, does not leave the ninety-nine in the wilderness, and go after the one which is lost, until he finds it? And when he has found it, lays it on his shoulders, rejoicing..." (Luke 15:3–7).

About to leave this earth, Jesus bequeathed his work of guidance and benevolence to his chosen followers. He appointed one to lead all the rest and everyone whom they would attract. This man was commissioned, not as a man of affairs, a soldier or a sage, but simply as a shepherd after Jesus' own example: "When they had finished breakfast, Jesus said to Simon Peter, 'Simon, son of John, do you

Jericho, a place of palms is thought to be the oldest city in the world. Here Jesus healed a blind man and visited the home of the publican Zacchaeus. In the foreground, archaeological excavations of a mound which is 10,000 years old.

130

love me more than these?' He said to him, 'Yes, Lord; you know that I love you.' He said to him, 'Feed my lambs.... Tend my sheep... Feed my sheep'" (John 21:15–17).

Finally, the great closing event of history, the universal judgment of men, is likewise described in the imagery of shepherding. Without violence, personalities are separated within the mass, as naturally as, in our own time in the Middle East, mixed herds are divided into two classes: "When the Son of man comes in his glory, and all the angels with him, then he will sit on his glorious throne. Before him will be gathered all the nations, and he will separate them one from another as a shepherd separates the sheep from the goats, and he will place the sheep at his right hand, but the goats at the left..." (Matthew 25:31–46).

WHERE BREAD WAS MULTIPLIED

One tradition places the miracle of the multiplication of the loaves and fishes in Jesus' favorite spot near Capernaum, Tabgha. The name is an abbreviation of the Greek word "Heptapegon": "Seven Springs." In Byzantine times, a church commemorating the wonder was built here and it was so beautifully ornamented — especially with floor mosaics — that many people of old considered it the most wonderful place of worship in the Holy Land. Relics of these mosaics can still be seen today: plants, birds and animals so vividly portrayed that they could come straight from the lake shore now. In the apse there is a basket, framed by two fishes, containing loaves of bread each marked with a cross. Under the altar there is a sacred stone, mentioned by the pilgrim Aetheria as the one on which Jesus had asked that the loaves and fishes be placed. In ancient times, such artistic designs were rarely created by one single individual, but were the result of deep religious impulse on the part of the community. These rich images testify to the fact that the miracle of the multiplication, when about five thousand people were fed with five barley loaves and two small fishes (John 6:3–11), must have made an enormous, lasting impression on the Christians.

Until now, history has tended to situate the event on the eastern shore of the lake. Ancient

Approaching Jerusalem from the Jordan Valley
and the east, travelers in ancient times first saw the
Holy City from the top of the Mount of Olives.
Jesus often looked down
at Jerusalem from this vantage point.

rules of worship, however, center the memory of different events in one locality, and so commemoration of the event may have been transferred to Tabgha. However, the most recent excavations (1968) tend to suggest that the uninhabited Tabgha Plain, so dear to Jesus, may well have been the actual spot, correctly represented still by the Church of the Multiplication. In any case, it is obvious that we are concerned not with a simple miracle but with a religious manifestation of unique importance. The atmosphere was one of political and devotional tension. John the Baptist had been executed during the year (29 A.D.) and Jesus could not risk going to Jerusalem for Passover. There, the Roman procurator, Pilate, had already massacred pilgrims from Galilee, in the forecourt of the temple, because he was afraid of imminent rebellion. In this time of intense messianic expectation, therefore, it is not surprising that the crowd wished to make Jesus their own messianic king and that he had difficulty in getting away from them (John 6:15).

BY THE POOL OF BETHESDA

Some time later, Jesus did go up to Jerusalem for "a feast of the Jews." This may well have been Shavuot (Pentecost), 29 A.D. Near the present St. Stephen's Gate (Lions Gate) there was a pool close to the so-called sheep market. Its water was said to have healing powers and so it was frequented by a multitude of invalids. It was here that Jesus healed a cripple with a word: "Rise, take up your pallet and walk" (John 5:8). Some Pharisees saw the healed man carrying his bed and accosted Jesus, because it was the sabbath, the day on which it was forbidden to carry anything. Jesus' answer was, "My Father is working still, and I am working" (John 5:17).

Their indignation turned into open hostility at Jesus' claim to being the son of God. They wanted to kill him and so the event became a turning point in his life. The place where it occurred was in itself of unique significance. Excavations have revealed the foundations of a Hellenistic-Roman thermal establishment with two different ponds which were once surrounded by five colonnades, as mentioned by John. There was no similar installation in the

"...there is in Jerusalem by the Sheep Gate a pool, in Hebrew called Bethzatha, which has five porticoes"

(John 5:2)

The Pool of Bethzatha (left) lay not far from the temple courtyard, but outside the city walls. There, on a sabbath day, Jesus healed a paralytic. Near the pool is St. Anne's Church (right), built by the Crusaders on a site which one tradition holds was the home of Joachim and Anne, Mary's parents.

area, so there is no doubt that this is one of the few places in Jerusalem where Jesus actually stood.

During the Byzantine period, a church with three naves was built above the place and its imposing substructure is still to be seen. Under the northern aisle, part of one of the pools has been preserved to commemorate the miracle in question. Next to it, ruins have been found of an old pagan place of worship, originally dedicated to a Semitic god and later to Asclepius, who was frequently worshiped near healing waters, as for example, in Tiberias and Gadara. Votive offerings, dating from the second century, provide further evidence as, for instance, a foot dedicated by one Pompeia Lucilia.

In connection with the pool of Bethesda, we are faced with the interesting fact that, during Jesus' lifetime, pagan rites were probably still being practiced on the edge of the city, though outside its walls. It further shows that the entire population of Jerusalem was by no means orthodox. There must have been very liberal groups also, and Herod himself must have belonged to one of these. Popular

beliefs always live on as undercurrents of official religion. Here, at Bethesda, they had gained the upper hand. Simple Jewish folk believed that an angel entered the pool and stirred the water, bestowing it with healing powers. According to the pagan belief, it was Asclepius who healed people while they slept after having bathed. Jesus always sought people in their own surroundings. For him, Bethesda was the place where ills and pains from all over the city were to be found. And he came in person to assuage them with his own words.

HARASSMENT OF JESUS

A group of Pharisees and officials from the Sanhedrin went up to Galilee to investigate "the case of Jesus." Their verdict: his performance of miracles is a fact but so is his disregard for laws of the Torah. He does not observe the precepts on the sabbath, purification rites or the fasts. Therefore, since he cannot be considered a prophet, his whole ministry must be based on deception and he must be a tool, even a helper, of the devil. The Torah is the measure of all, and anyone who rebels

137

"'Go, wash in the pool of Siloam' ... he went and washed and came back seeing" *(John 9:7)*

Another famous pool in Jerusalem is the pool of Siloam. There Jesus sent a man, blind from birth, to wash in the waters. The man's eyes were healed, and for first time he saw himself reflected in the water.

against it is guilty of heresy. As is well known from Jewish writings, there were very severe penalties for this: "He who offends, knowingly and intentionally, against the laws concerning the sabbath or against any other commandment of the Torah, is impious. He must be warned and, if he pays no heed and continues to violate the commandments of the Torah, he must be condemned to death and stoned."

Rebellion against the clergy in Jerusalem and defamation, or desecration, of the temple are punishable by death. Anyone who claims for himself divine honors or powers is impious. Anyone who knowingly blasphemes has to be arrested and may be convicted on the evidence of reliable witnesses. Anyone convicted of blasphemy must be stoned. After he has been stoned to death, his body shall be hung upon a tree. In the late afternoon on the day of the execution, the body shall be taken down and buried before dusk. A false prophet preaches abomination and tries to lead Israel to apostasy by means of dreams, visions, false prophecies, magic, conjuring up the dead, hallucinations and true miracles. He will most likely be considered a tool of the devil and

must be tried by the Sanhedrin and, if condemned, must be executed in Jerusalem.

The situation had become threatening. As soon as he became suspect, and the authorities began to show an interest in him, Jesus was deserted by many. But, when he asked his twelve disciples whether they also wanted to abandon him, Peter plainly acknowledged his belief in the messianic mission of Jesus (John 6:67–69). To avoid being declared outlaws, the population of Capernaum also deserted him. It is typical of close Oriental family ties that his relatives (Joseph was probably already dead) tried, in vain, to save him by declaring that he was not responsible (Mark 3:21).

In Nazareth's synagogue, a disturbance occurred when he interpreted a prophecy of Isaiah (61:1) as referring to himself, thus proclaiming himself the Messiah (Luke 4:29). His apparently arrogant manner and lack of proof for his claim so inflamed those present that they drove him to the edge of a hill, to throw him down and afterward, if necessary, to stone him for blasphemy. Actually this did not happen, because Jesus somehow evaded them. The event must have occurred on one

The pool of Siloam is supplied by the spring of Gihon by means of a channel 1,750 feet long cut through the rock by King Hezekiah.

of Nazareth's hillocks. Luke failed to provide exact details of Jesus' escape and so popular imagination was given free rein. In the time of the Crusaders, a hill about a mile and a half from the town was known as the Mount of the Precipitation. It was said that Jesus had jumped from there across a deep gully onto a cliff which was supposed to bear the imprint of his feet and garments. Under it was a cave in which Mary was thought to have hidden in fear. The memory of this latter tradition is still preserved in the Chapel of Our Lady of the Fright, situated quite close to the town.

Following this event, Jesus did not return to Nazareth. He began to lead a wanderer's existence: "Foxes have holes and birds of the air have nests; but the Son of man has nowhere to lay his head" (Luke 9:58).

At first, he remained in southern Galilee where he again met the Sanhedrin delegation and was questioned by them about the ritual washing of hands and the validity of the Torah (Matthew 15:1-4). They also asked for a sign. Jesus' answers became more and more pointed, and he warned his disciples to beware of agitators. For the first time, he crossed the borders of his country, toward Tyre and Sidon in Phoenicia. Tyre was noted for its magnificent necropolis. It also had the right to mint its own coinage, and its silver drachma was valid in the Jerusalem temple. Usually, Jesus stressed that he had been sent exclusively to the lost sheep of Israel, and that only after his death was the Gospel to reach the whole world. Now, however, he made a notable exception and healed the daughter of a woman of Canaan because of the great faith she demonstrated in him (Matthew 15:22–28).

"Now a certain man was ill, Lazarus of Bethany, the village of Mary and her sister Martha" (John 11:1)

Jesus often visited Bethany near Jerusalem (right). Here he restored to life his friend Lazarus who had been dead for some days. The Arabic name of the locality is still El-'Azariyeh. Nuns in white veils (left) visit the Church of Lazarus in Bethany.

CHAPTER 7 WORDS AND DEEDS

In which Jesus points the way to Christianity

On the Day of Atonement, Jesus was in the neighborhood of Caesarea Philippi, at the foot of Mount Hermon. Here is to be found one of the sources of the Jordan, welling up from a deep grotto dedicated to the god Pan, originally named after him, today known as Banias. Here Jesus questioned his disciples as to what people thought the Son of man was. Peter answered: "You are the Christ, the Son of the living God" (Matthew 16:16).

PRIMACY

Then Jesus spoke the famous words: "Blessed are you, Simon Bar-Jona! For flesh and blood has not revealed this to you, but my Father who is in heaven. And I tell you, you are Peter, and on this rock I will build my church, and the powers of death shall not prevail against it. I will give you the keys of the kingdom of heaven, and whatever you bind on earth shall be bound in heaven, and whatever you loose on earth shall be loosed in heaven" (Matthew 16:17–19).

This is the promise of the primacy which all Peter's successors shall inherit from him. As Abraham is the rock upon which God built

the world, so Peter is the foundation upon which Jesus builds his church — a new edifice and not a special branch of the ancient people. The bunch of keys is the sign of the steward, the representative of the landlord himself. The image is taken from everyday life, for the Holy Land is a country of keys. The Church of the Holy Sepulchre, for instance, is still locked and unlocked with solemn ceremony, even today. The door of the synagogue of the Samaritans has three separate locks, the keys to which are in the hands of three different stewards.

Not far from Caesarea Philippi is the second source of the Jordan, Dan, used in the common Old Testament phrase "from Dan to Beersheba," indicating the most northerly point in the land of Canaan, Beersheba being the southern point. Dan was also a town of the tribe of this name. An imposing gateway, a citadel dating from the time of the kingdom of Israel, and many Roman remains have been found there. Although Dan is not mentioned in the New Testament, it is likely that Jesus visited the place. The proximity of Dan to Caesarea Philippi (whether by chance or

"When he (Jesus) had said this, he cried with a loud voice, 'Lazarus, come out'" (John 11:43)

The flight of stairs leading down to the tomb of Lazarus. The grave was carved out of the rock of the hillside.

"Jesus said to her, 'I am the resurrection and the life'"

(John 11:25)

The Church of Lazarus, Bethany, in its lower half, recalls Lazarus lying in the tomb and Jesus' promise: "I am the resurrection and the life."

design) shows, in its own way, that Christianity was a new experience in the world. It was at this time that Jesus withdrew from the crowds and concentrated entirely on instructing his disciples, preparing them for the difficult events they would have to face: "From that time Jesus began to show his disciples that he must go to Jerusalem and suffer many things from the elders and chief priests and scribes, and be killed, and on the third day be raised" (Matthew 16:21).

ON MOUNT TABOR

A week later, Jesus ascended a high mountain, taking with him his most faithful disciples, Peter, James and John. They were also soon to accompany him in Gethsemane. Perhaps the mountain was Hermon; possibly, as Byzantine tradition suggests, Mount Tabor, which stands isolated in a plain. It may have been some other mountain — we cannot be sure. There the disciples had a vision of the glory of the Messiah. Its purpose was to help them remember it, while awaiting the resurrection of the Son of man.

The experience was a unique manifestation:

"And he was transfigured before them, and his face shone like the sun, and his garments became white as light. And behold, there appeared to them Moses and Elijah, talking with him. And Peter said to Jesus, 'Lord, it is well that we are here; if you wish, I will make three booths here, one for you, and one for Moses, and one for Elijah.' He was still speaking, when lo, a bright cloud overshadowed them, and a voice from the cloud said, 'This is my beloved Son, with whom I am well pleased; listen to him'" (Matthew 17:2–5).

A modern church on Mount Tabor, built in Syrian style upon the ruins of a Crusader church, reflects the wonderful mystery it commemorates in its mosaics and chapels, especially beautiful in the reflection of light when sunshine penetrates the interior. The view from the mountain top is unique. Even more imposing is the effect at dawn or dusk, with the sun rising in the east, behind the main mosaic of the church, or setting in the blood-red sky of the west. The panorama takes in the whole of Galilee from the hills of Samaria to Mount Hermon, and from the Carmel range to Lake Kinnereth. The lake waters

147

The village of Bethany lies at the foot of the Mount of Olives. For thousands of years, its inhabitants have been engaged in the production of olive oil. This press (left) dates from the Middle Ages, but in Jesus' time much the same technique was used. Bethany, old and new (right): the ruins of a Crusader tower and a modern Greek Orthodox church.

flash mysteriously when touched by the rays of the rising sun. Among the many towns and hamlets in the surrounding area is Nain, where Jesus restored to life the only son of a widow (Luke 7:11).

AT THE FEAST OF TABERNACLES

Jesus was very fond of the liturgy. However, when he went to Jerusalem for the feast of Tabernacles, in 29 A.D., the situation was very tense. People were discussing him and opinions were divided. During the service, while the priests, with willow branches, were circling the altar of the burnt offering in procession, and the high priest was sprinkling water from the pool of Siloam, Jesus exclaimed in a high voice: "If anyone thirst, let him come to me and drink. He who believes in me, as the scripture has said, 'Out of his heart shall flow rivers of living water'" (John 7:37–38).

It is likely that, while the temple was illuminated by festal torches, he spoke the words: "I am the light of the world; he who follows me will not walk in darkness, but will have the light of life" (John 8:12).

During these days, an episode took place of

"And seeing a fig tree ... (Jesus) found nothing on it but leaves only. And he said to it, 'May no fruit ever come from you again'" (Matthew 21:19)

Jesus' pardoning a woman guilty of adultery. He was empowered by God to do so (John 8:6–11). This incident drew a great deal of attention to Jesus. The police were actually sent to arrest him but "no one laid hands on him" (John 7:44). When the high priests asked the officers why they did not carry out their orders, the answer was: "No man ever spoke like this man" (John 7:46).

BY THE POOL OF SILOAM

Let us imagine ourselves standing by the pool of Siloam, south of Jerusalem in the Valley of the Cheesemakers (Tyropaeon). All around are flowering orchards and terraced plots. Here the gardens of Solomon flourished at one time. On the ground lie pieces of broken columns, relics of the past. Arab women are washing clothes, children are playing in the water — an idyllic scene. On Fridays, especially, men and women can be seen in the shadow of the minaret, pouring water over themselves in solemn ceremony, seeking a cure from some disease.

To this day, Moslems still tend to revere the pool as a holy place the way Christians once did. Not far from here, Jesus healed a blind man and then, to test his faith, sent him to wash in the pool. Subsequently, the authorities started an investigation, summoning the man whom Jesus had healed. It was confirmed that a cure had taken place but, again, Jesus had violated the sabbath laws. The dignitaries would not admit that he had performed a miracle, and charged him with blasphemy. Furthermore, those who believed in him were also punishable. The authorities wanted to set an example to serve as a warning to others, and the man, who had been healed, was cast out of the community. He was forbidden to do any business or have social relationships with other people. Thus, the conflict between Jesus and his enemies was nearing its climax. On this occasion, Jesus revealed himself as the Son of man to the patient whom he had cured, an ordinary man who, in turn, acknowledged Jesus for what he was (John 9:1–39).

JESUS, THE SHEPHERD

The following December, during the feast

of the Dedication of the Temple, Jesus was walking in Solomon's Porch when he was asked if he were the Messiah. He replied in terms of one of his favorite parables: "I told you, and you do not believe. The works that I do in my Father's name, they bear witness to me; but you do not believe, because you do not belong to my sheep. My sheep hear my voice, and I know them, and they follow me; and I give them eternal life, and they shall never perish, and no one shall snatch them out of my hand. My Father, who has given them to me, is greater than all, and no one is able to snatch them out of the Father's hand. I and the Father are one" (John 10:25–30).

When he had finished speaking, people threw stones at him, not because he had said he was the Messiah but because they considered he had blasphemed by referring to himself as God. Christian art first pictured Jesus as the good shepherd. It was not an idyllic image, as was proven by its reference to the final outcome of Jesus' struggle. It infers the twofold nature of his character: he is strong and valiant in defense of his position against all his opponents, yet he is charitable and tender to those in his care. Jesus avoided his enemies on this occasion, and returned to the place from which he had once started out, the banks of the Jordan where he was baptized, where he had first preached and where he had attracted many followers (John 10:40).

IN BETHANY

Bethany lies on the southeastern slope of the Mount of Olives, on the edge of the desert. In Jesus' time, it was an isolated and peaceful place, not divided by the modern road to Jericho. It was one of Jesus' favorite spots. On his walks along the Mount of Olives, he often called at the house of Lazarus, where his sisters, Mary and Martha, lived. The evangelists describe three of his visits, of which one became world famous because of the raising of Lazarus whose name is perpetuated in the name of the modern Arabic village of El-'Azariyeh. The brother had died and the sisters sent for Jesus. His disciples tried to dissuade him from returning to a district where his life was threatened, but he was insistent. Thomas, the twin, was the first to say that all of them ought to share his fate: "Let us also go, that we may die with him" (John 11:16).

John's description of subsequent events is so graphic and tender that it cannot fail to move the reader deeply. When Jesus and his company arrived, Lazarus was dead and buried. At the house there was a crowd of mourners. Outside the village proper, Jesus met Martha and, in the conversation which followed, this simple woman became inspired. Even in the depth of her grief, she recognized the light in Jesus: "Yes, Lord; I believe that you are the Christ, the Son of God, he who is coming into the world" (John 11:27).

Mary came to join them. She was weeping so hard that she could not speak. Together they went to the graveside. Jesus, too, was deeply moved and wept. He asked that the stone sealing the grave be removed, said a prayer of thanksgiving to God, then called out with a loud voice: "Lazarus, come out." The dead man came out, his hands and feet bound with bandages, and his face wrapped with a cloth. Jesus said to them, "Unbind him, and let him go" (John 11:43–44).

The tomb was a typical one, carved out of the rock, containing an antechamber and a burial chamber in which the dead lay on a slab of rock. The modern Latin church nearby is built in the shape of a mausoleum. Its fine mosaics emphasize the words spoken by Jesus to Martha: "I am the resurrection and the life; he who believes in me, though he die, yet shall live, and whoever lives and believes in me shall never die" (John 11:25–26). These words are said at every Christian funeral.

THE MEANING OF THE MIRACLES

"My speech and my message were not in plausible words of wisdom, but in demonstration of the Spirit and power." These words could well have been spoken by Jesus, though they were later written by an apostle (1 Corinthians 2:4). Constantly interwoven with reports of what Jesus said, the Gospels relate stories of miracles — striking acts of extraordinary power. These have been explained individually, in various ways, by modern commentators; some authors have tried to discredit them. But, they will not disappear from our reading of the Gospel for the simple reason that, if we discard them entirely, we

"And he said to them, 'When you pray, say: Father, hallowed be thy name. Thy kingdom come'" *(Luke 11:2)*

On the Mount of Olives, Jesus taught his disciples many things including the Lord's Prayer. To commemorate his role as teacher, the church and monastery of "Pater Noster" were erected. In the cloister (left), the prayer is written in forty-four languages. In Norwegian and Aramaic (below).

"'I am the vine, you are the branches. He who abides in me, and I in him, he it is that bears much fruit...'"

(John 15:5)

In Jerusalem Jesus spoke the parable of the vine. In olden times, there were many vineyards and wine presses in the Holy Land. The vine is thus a frequent symbol in the Bible.

tear the web of the Gospel story beyond salvage and destroy the only detailed source of the life of Jesus which is in existence: no miracles, no Gospel.

The wonders of the Gospel narrative are not simply magic tricks. Jesus is no mere magician. The miracles have their own language and this is no arbitrary invention. The message of the signs was considered quite early in the Christian story, and a "book of signs" interpreting them was soon written: the Gospel according to John. This work provides us with clues to many other miracle stories transmitted by the other evangelists. An analytical study was published by a modern scholar, C. H. Dodd, to whom every reader of the Gospels is indebted *(Interpretation of the Fourth Gospel.* Cambridge University Press, 1953).

The symbolism of seven great miracles by Jesus in person is spelled out at length in John's Gospel by means of discourses or monologues which accompany them. First, we have the miracle at Cana: wine for water. The full water pots represent the entire system of Jewish ceremonial and a religion founded

"...'Go into the village opposite, where on entering you will find a colt tied... untie it and bring it here'"

(Luke 19:30)

From the village of Bethpage (left) Jesus rode on an ass to a triumphal welcome in Jerusalem. This Gospel event is commemorated each year by the Latin Church's Palm Sunday procession. A fresco in Bethpage chapel (right) depicts the Gospel story.

on the level of intense efforts for purification in God's eyes. Jesus changes this into something positive and superior, a religion based on a higher level, that of the truth, grace and glory of God himself. Therefore, the Cana wonder represents a firm Christian principle: the Law was given by Moses. Grace and truth came through Jesus Christ (John 1:17). So, at Cana, the glory of Jesus is shown for the first time by the sign of water changed into wine, a symbol that, with his coming, the old order is transformed into something new (John 2:1–11).

At Capernaum, Jesus restored to health the son of an official, who was at the point of death. At Bethesda, in Jerusalem, he healed a thirty-eight-year-old cripple by the side of the pool. This man, too, was almost as good as dead. The symbolism of both miracles is that Jesus, with a word, can rescue human life from the immediate threat of death and destruction. The water symbolism of Bethesda connects with that of Cana. In the village, Jesus enhanced human life by offering a new religion. The two cures show that he is capable of healing and sustaining life, even

though it is almost at an end (John 4:46–5:9).

By the lakeside in Galilee, Jesus performed the long-remembered miracle of the multiplication of the loaves and fishes. Soon after, he walked on the very waters of the lake, to come to the rescue of his terrified disciples (John 6:1–21). The meaning of the feeding is explained at great length, in the Gospel of John, in the discourse which follows, but it is supplemented by the water miracle also. Briefly, Jesus is another Moses who provides extraordinary nourishment, valid not only for earthly existence but productive of eternal life as well. He is also lord of the storm, independent of the elements of nature, and, as such, able to communicate life and well-being through means quite different from the ordinary. So, Jesus is able not only to heal a dying body. He can positively sustain life, naturally and supernaturally.

In Jerusalem, near the pool of Siloam, Jesus healed a man blind from birth. As is evident from the accompanying discourses, the symbolism is that of light triumphant over darkness. The recurrence of the water theme provides a clue to the detail inherent in

"when he drew near and saw the city he wept over it"
(Luke 19:41)

the message. As men are reborn to life
(through baptism), so they receive the true
light which Jesus supplies. As water was once
turned into wine at Cana, so the water of
Siloam is effective if it is given power by
one sent out by God: Jesus. This theme of
light leads on to a distinction between those
who follow Christ and those who prefer the
darkness, in this case, Jesus' opponents in
Jerusalem (John 9).

At Bethany, Jesus performed the most
impressive of his wonders by raising Lazarus
from the grave. The symbolism completes the
picture of Jesus as the Lord of life and death.
Not only can he enhance human existence
and strengthen life, when it is almost ex-
tinguished, he can also restore it after it has
been definitely lost. In detail, eternal life can
be enjoyed here and now by those who
respond to the word of Christ. Moreover,
Christ has power, after the death of the body,
to raise the dead to renewed existence in the
world beyond the grave (John 11).

The Bethany motif — death, anointing,
burial and return from the tomb — leads on
to the greatest miracle in the Gospel, the
return of Jesus himself from the grave.
Logically, this wonder is given the longest
explanation of all the "signs" in the Fourth
Gospel through five long chapters *preceding*
the events themselves: how Jesus is to be put
to death, his legacy to his loved ones, how he
will come back, how he will live on in the
hearts of believers, how he will be venerated
in the Church and in the world, even till the
end of time (John 13–17).

"And the crowds that went before him and that followed

im shouted, 'Hosanna to the Son of David!...Hosanna...'"

(Matthew 21:9)

Nuns carry the *lulav* (palm frond) and sing "Hosanna to the Son of David" (left). This annual procession marks the beginning of the Holy Week for the Latin Church. The procession crosses the Kidron valley and enters the walls of Jerusalem through St. Stephen's Gate, ending in the courtyard of St. Anne's Church (below).

CHAPTER 8 WANTED

In which Jesus is a fugitive

The raising of Lazarus had serious consequences for Jesus. The religious authorities thought that the episode involved the practice of magic or conjuring. A special meeting of the Sanhedrin was called. The members were faced with a dilemma: on the one hand, the people had been tremendously impressed by the miracle; on the other, there was the danger that the Romans would intervene if the messianic movement should spread: "If we let him go on thus, everyone will believe in him, and the Romans will come and destroy both our holy place and our nation" (John 11:48).

The acting high priest, Caiaphas, urged them to make a decision: "You know nothing at all; you do not understand that it is expedient for you that one man should die for the people, and that the whole nation should not perish.... So from that day on they took counsel how to put him to death" (John 11:49–53).

For forty days, a herald was given the responsibility of proclaiming to the population that anyone knowing the whereabouts of Jesus should at once notify the authorities so that he might be arrested (John 11:57; cf. Sanhedrin 43a). This happened in February of 30 A.D. Jesus did not surrender himself immediately, because he wanted to meet death as a paschal lamb, at Passover feast time. At first, he lingered in Ephraim (the present Et-Taijiba), isolated in the hills, about twelve miles from Jerusalem, amid fertile olive groves. Ephraim affords a magnificent view of the Judaean Desert and the Jordan Valley. Most likely, Jesus had been there many times before. Evidence that this was one of Jesus' favorite spots is provided by the ruins of a Byzantine church with a baptismal font, carried over into modern times, with the generally Christian atmosphere of the village and its three churches.

During the week preceding Passover, Jesus moved down to Jericho. He would have passed by the site of the ancient fortified city which was destroyed by Joshua. In Jesus' time this would have laid buried in a hill, only recently examined by modern excavators. The newer Jericho spread south of it across the plain "covering it with dwellings and an abundance of fruit trees and palms," as the ancient writer Strabo described it. The generous spring (which Elisha the prophet had turned from brackish to sweet) was channeled through the soil to create fertile fields and gardens. Jericho was the site of Herod's winter palace and, like him, many affluent citizens lived here in houses decorated with mosaics, among them being the tax collector, Zacchaeus, whose house Jesus visited (Luke 19:1–10). As he was leaving the town he was greeted as the Messiah by a blind man who called him "Jesus, son of David" (Mark 10:47), and Jesus healed him.

Deliberately, Jesus chose the route which climbs from the Jordan Valley to Jerusalem. By the Jordan River, the boundary of the Holy Land, he had begun his ministry which was about to reach its climax in the Passion. He was joined by many pilgrims as he ascended the Roman road through Wadi Kelt, past the spot where, today, the Greek monastery Choziba clings to the cliff face. It was founded during Byzantine times in honor of Mary. The wild ravines and the hills of bright red rock, giving the impression in some places of being covered with blood, were the setting for the parable of the Good Samaritan. Now Jesus spoke somberly of the present journey: "Behold, we are going up to Jerusalem; and the Son of man will be delivered to the chief priests and the scribes, and they will condemn him to death, and deliver him to the Gentiles; and they will mock him, and spit upon him, and scourge him, and kill him; and after three days he will rise" (Mark 10:33–34).

In Bethany, Mary, Lazarus' sister, humbly anointed his feet as he sat at supper, causing Judas to make the tactless remark that the money might have been better used for the poor. The evangelist comments: "This he said, not that he cared for the poor but because he was a thief, and as he had the money box he used to take what was put into it" (John 12:6).

PALM SUNDAY

Jesus climbed the Mount of Olives, the place of revelation. According to Ezekiel, the glory of the Lord would be manifest here (11:23), and Zechariah prophesied that the feet of God would stand upon it during a tremendous manifestation of himself (14:4).

On Mount Zion three religions meet.
The tomb of David is sacred to Jews and
Moslems. In the same precincts
was the scene of Jesus' Last Supper.

Because they thought that Jesus would intervene politically on their behalf, the pilgrims came out of the town with palm branches to meet the Messiah, acclaiming him and escorting him in solemn procession. Somewhere near Bethphage, however, he mounted an ass, thus hinting that he was not a heroic warrior entering his capital on a charger, but the Prince of Peace bringing salvation in gentleness and humility, without battle cries or force of arms. Within the Bethphage chapel there is a rock, dating from Crusader times, depicting this scene in frescos. The traditional, liturgical Palm Sunday procession has engraved it indelibly on the hearts of the faithful. On the lid of an ossuary, there is mention of Galileans, which is of special interest since it may shed some light on the ease with which the apostles were able to procure the ass for Jesus' triumphal entry. Bethphage may have been a Galilean settlement, and we might suppose that the family of Lazarus in Bethany was also of Galilean origin. Thus, in the area, Jesus was able to contact compatriots.

When Jesus reached the top of the Mount of Olives, he saw the city spread before him, its temple, towers and walls all radiant in the sunshine. Then he "wept over it, saying 'Would that even today you knew the things that make for peace! But now they are hid from your eyes. For the days shall come upon you, when your enemies will cast up a bank about you and surround you, and hem you in on every side, and dash you to the ground, you and your children within you, and they will not leave one stone upon another in you; because you did not know the time of your visitation'" (Luke 19:41–44).

The words contrast sharply with the joy of the crowd around Jesus, yet no one familiar with the many contradictions inherent in this country and its people will be surprised. Not far away, the scene is commemorated by the small chapel of Dominus Flevit ("The Lord Wept"), one of the most beautiful in the vicinity of Jerusalem. The view extends across the deep Valley of Kidron to the Temple Mount and the Aqsa Mosque. Beyond it, one can see the black cupola of the Church of the Holy Sepulchre and the modern tower of the Lutheran Church of the Redeemer. The

"'The Teacher says..., Where is the guest room, where I am to eat the passover with my disciples?'" *(Luke 22:11)*

Dormition Abbey, also, is quite clearly visible. The whole city nestles in the surrounding hills, stretching from Ramat Rachel to the Tomb of Samuel. The height itself, which affords this view, bears traces of bygone history: the ancient tombs of the Jebusites (one of which contained a scarab of the Egyptian Pharaoh Tutmose III, who reigned more than a thousand years before Christ) and Jewish tombs dating from the time of Jesus. There are also the remains of a Byzantine church and monastery which were decorated with mosaics. A chapel has recently been erected on the ancient remains and provides an example of Italian church architecture. Its wrought-iron windows recall the mystery of Christian faith with a representation of the chalice and the crown of thorns. Here, the deeper meaning of the "visitation," mentioned by Jesus, suddenly becomes clear. There is question not only of a judgment bringing total destruction but also of a blessing which has allowed new life to grow out of old.

Jesus must have followed the ancient Roman road which lead up from Jericho

The Cenacle (in Latin *Coenaculum:* "Dining Room") is in the upper floor of this building. Here Jesus and his disciples ate the Last Supper.

170

"And he will show you a large... room furnished; there make ready"

(Luke 22:12)

In this large room, the Last Supper was taken, according to old belief. One Byzantine column still stands in the Crusader reconstruction. The slender pillar in the left-rear corner bears a medieval capital with the Pelican-Christ motif.

along the mountain ridge, down into the valley, then up to the city. It is no longer possible to trace this route. A ninth-century tradition has it that Jesus entered the temple area through the Golden Gate, reserved in ancient times for the priests. The Sultan Suleiman ordered it walled up so that no one should pass through until the return of Christ. The rejoicing of pilgrims long ago is today echoed by the voice of children who line the processional route. In the Middle East, people compare the stammering of a child with the speech of a prophet, his stuttering with that of a saint.

During the next few days of his last week, Jesus went to the temple daily to heal the sick and to preach. To his enemies, he was a thorn in the flesh. They did not dare arrest him, however, in the surrounding crowd of pilgrims. So, they tried to engage him in all sorts of controversies in order to trap him. For example, they asked his opinion as to whether or not taxes should be paid to the emperor. But Jesus was too intelligent to allow himself to be compromised. Soon afterward the chief priests, the scribes and the

"And they led Jesus to the high priest . . ." (Mark 14:53)

By this road Jesus descended from Mount Zion, across the Kidron Valley to Gethsemane. Remains of the ancient stepped road dating from Maccabean times can still be seen near the Church of St. Peter in Gallicantu (Cockcrow) commemorating Peter's repentance after the triple denial of his Master.

elders assembled in the house of the high priest, Caiaphas, to work out a scheme. They decided first to capture him by fraud, and then kill him. Judas, who had probably been acting as informer on Jesus and his disciples for some time, offered his services in return for thirty pieces of silver. The tragic figure of this man can be understood only against the background of the uncertain destiny which surrounds all human beings.

THE LAST SUPPER

The festival of Passover with its Seder celebration was approaching. Of old, the observance of holy days was considered so important that several different calendars were in use. This is illustrated by the practice of Christians in the East today. Therefore, the date of Passover varied. According to John and the Qumran sources, it would seem that Jesus and his disciples celebrated the festival a few days before the "official" date. The house where this took place is not known. It may have been anywhere in the maze of streets in the Old City. The name of the host is also unknown. This is not surprising in a country where so much stress is put on hospitality and where families open their doors to pilgrims and strangers, especially on Seder night. The hall shown today as the place of the Last Supper was built in Gothic style by Franciscans, in the fourteenth century. It is the site where the primitive Christian community used to assemble before Pentecost. As a result, earlier and later events have been brought together here. Is not the very obscurity which surrounds this place a reminder of that holy night which was illumined by the light of Christ in a special way?

Jesus, with his faith firmly rooted in the religious traditions of his people, celebrated a true Seder. This, however, acquired a new meaning through the personality of Jesus, which is emphasized by the evangelists.

Before commencing, the head of the family washes his hands. Though not mentioned by the Gospel writers, it is likely that a recital of the story of the Exodus of the Israelites from Egypt followed. This evoked spontaneous questions and answers between the head of the family and the youngest person present,

175

From the Grotto of the Betrayal
Jesus went out to meet his captors.
Restored to something like its
original form, it still shows inscriptions
dating from the twelfth century.

The Basilica of the Agony was built in
1924 on Byzantine and Crusader
remains. The mosaic represents
Christ's offering up to his Father his
sufferings and those of the world.

"...he said to his disciples, 'Sit here, while I go yonder and pray'"

(Matthew 26:36)

Twelve domes in the ceiling of the Basilica of the Agony and other ornaments in the church recall the names of sixteen generous nations, hence its modern name "Church of All Nations."

probably John. The bitter herbs, the bread of affliction and, above all, the imminent betrayal by Judas provided Jesus with the opportunity to allude to his own Passion: "'Truly, truly, I say to you, one of you will betray me.... It is he to whom I shall give this morsel when I have dipped it.' So when he had dipped the morsel, he gave it to Judas, the son of Simon Iscariot" (John 13:21, 26).

According to ancient custom, the head of the family offers the first mouthful to one of those present as a sign of an especially close friendship. Therein lies the great tragedy, as this gesture, in that instance, became a symbol of deep division. Jesus offered the bitter herbs to the person who would betray him. Soon afterward, Judas left the table. Next, as the Seder procedure demands, Jesus took the unleavened bread, symbolizing, according to ancient tradition, the people of Israel. Then he spoke the decisive new words: "Take, eat; this is my body."

When the cup of grace was passed, he said, "Drink of it, all of you; for this is my blood of the covenant" (Matthew 26:26–27).

The celebration had been transformed by

"…the soldiers plaited a crown of thorns, and put it on his head, and arrayed him in a purple robe" *(John 19:2)*

During his trial, Jesus was crowned with thorns. Christians view such a crown as symbolic, as is evident in the dome of the shrine of the Flagellation (left).
A variety of rugged thorns (right) is still found among the flora of the Holy Land.

the fact that Jesus offered himself to his disciples. The theme of remembrance which had dominated the traditional Seder acquired a deeper meaning through Jesus. The blood which was about to be spilled would effect the salvation of all mankind. After the meal, Jesus and his company remained in serious conversation, discussing in great detail the close relationship between the master and his disciples. Jesus presented his parable of the vine: "I am the vine, you are the branches. He who abides in me, and I in him, he it is that bears much fruit, for apart from me you can do nothing…. If you abide in me, and my words abide in you, ask whatever you will and it shall be done for you" (John 15:5, 7).

Everyone present had the feeling that this was a leave-taking. After praying to his Father in heaven, Jesus arose from the dining table and went down with his disciples through the Valley of Kidron to Gethsemane. They had to remain in the Jerusalem area on account of the Passover festival.

GETHSEMANE
In the valley there was an olive orchard with

183

"and they bound him and led him away and delivered him to Pilate the governor"

(Matthew 27:2)

A dome topped by a cross stands over the traditional site of Lithostratos, the flagstone courtyard of the Roman fortress Antonia. Here Jesus is said to have been tried by the Roman governor, Pontius Pilate.

185

"Then he handed him over to them to be crucified"

(John 19:16)

After Jesus was scourged, Pilate had him led out in full view of the watching crowd and said, "Ecce Homo" — "Here is the man." The archway (below) in the interior of the Basilica Ecce Homo is prolonged outside in the Via Dolorosa by a similar arch, which bears the name Ecce Homo today. Sisters of Zion in prayer in the Basilica (right). Behind the altar the Roman archway frames the apse.

an oil press. It probably belonged to one of Jesus' friends. Following the Seder, the rest of the night is called "watch night," expressing the idea that, since God had decisively saved his people, they should keep watch into the late hours of this night. Accordingly, Jesus took only his closest friends, Peter, James and John, and asked them to keep watch with him while he went farther on and prayed. About a stone's throw away he knelt down and pleaded: "Abba, Father, all things are possible to thee; remove this cup from me." But, in the same way as throughout his whole ministry he had submitted to the will of God, so now he also prayed: "Yet not what I will, but what thou wilt" (Mark 14:36).

He stood up and went to seek comfort among his friends, only to discover that they had dozed off. He asked Simon, "Could you not watch one hour? Watch and pray that you may not enter into temptation" (Mark 14:37–38).

Three times Jesus returned to his friends seeking some comfort, but in the meantime he sweated blood, a token of the life-blood he would soon pour out upon the cross. His

mainstay was the message of an angel (inspiration from on high) assuring him that his blood would not be shed in vain but would serve for the redemption of others.

Meanwhile, the group coming to arrest him drew nearer. Roman soldiers armed with swords and Jewish guardians of the temple, carrying clubs and staves were led by Judas to Jesus' favorite spot in Gethsemane. The traitor greeted Jesus in front of the grotto with a kiss, symbolic of peace in the Middle East, in order to identify Jesus to his enemies. He declined to resist and allowed himself to be led away. His disciples, with two exceptions, fled immediately.

In the Garden of Gethsemane to this day there are eight hoary olive trees. They look as if they are petrified with age but young shoots sprout forth from them still, a symbol of the "watch night." They provide shade for the nearby Basilica of the Agony, a modern church resting on foundations of preceding places of worship built by the Byzantines and the Crusaders. Its windows of translucent alabaster veil the interior with a purple half-light, symbolic of mourning. In front of its altar lies the naked rock on which Jesus is said to have prayed.

QUESTIONS ON THE TRIAL AND SENTENCE

The legal proceedings against Jesus were among the shortest, most dramatic and most momentous in world history. The detailed reports in the four Gospels indicate the importance of the trial and also its authenticity. Some details remain uncertain because each of the evangelists has selected material which seemed most important to him, and highlighted the personality of Jesus from his particular point of view. Under the circumstances, we can provide only tentative conclusions regarding a number of problems which are outlined here.

Jesus was crucified on a Friday in the year 30 A.D., indicating that his public ministry must have lasted two years and some months. John expressly states that the execution took place on the day before Passover. The other evangelists give the impression that his trial was a very hasty affair, conducted within twenty-four hours, with sittings starting early and ending late. Yet, it has to be borne in mind that the writers of these summaries were not particularly interested in various phases of the trial but only in its outcome — the death of their Lord. Jesus may have followed one special calendar for the Passover celebration which meant that the "Last Supper" took place on the Tuesday of the previous week. This would have left two full days for the trial, if John was referring to the Passover celebrated according to the official reckoning used in the temple. In this uncertainty, we are face to face with Eastern ideology which, even in this matter of reading the phases of the moon, is guided by personal observations.

One question which intrigues many people in our own times is: Who was responsible for Jesus' death sentence? The supreme court of the Jews — the Sanhedrin — carried out a preliminary hearing. Most likely, it did not pronounce a sentence of death. Instead, it reached a decision to hand Jesus over to Pilate and to accuse him of a crime which carried the death penalty. This would oblige the procurator himself to take charge of the hearing. The accusation was based on Jesus'

claim to be the Messiah, which was interpreted as blasphemy, but it also implied political undertones. The Romans were suspicious of all messianic movements, and there was the danger that, given the occasion, their occupying forces might interfere with Jewish privileges. The religious aspect of the charge against Jesus was stressed, both before the Sanhedrin and Pilate, but its political consequences were also brought out. It should be borne in mind that both elements, religious and political, were, undoubtedly, contributing factors in the conviction.

Recently, it has been suggested that the whole process of the trial should be re-examined, to see if there were legal shortcomings. Yet, aside from the fact that a new trial can never be considered (no official documents of the original process exist), we have no reason to find fault with the proceedings from a legal point of view.

For religiously minded people, however, these questions are of minor importance. The trial of Jesus shows how, amid human weakness and frailty, God's intentions are realized: "Was it not necessary that the Christ

There are many caves to the east of Lithostratos and along the Way of the Cross (Via Dolorosa). The Greek Orthodox community believes that one was the prison cell of Christ or perhaps of Barabbas.

should suffer these things and enter into his glory?" (Luke 24:26). Jesus is the suffering servant of God, whose coming Isaiah the prophet foretold.

Throughout his public ministry, Jesus had many disputes with the Pharisees. During his trial, however, it was the opposition of the Sadducees which became more pronounced. They were officially in charge of the temple and were concerned with keeping up their good relationship with the Romans. Yet, all parties were represented at the decisive session of the Sanhedrin, so that no segment could be absolved from responsibility for its decisions. As usual, there were a few opportunists among them, but most of the participants were driven by zeal to do God's work, as they saw it. This fervor, from which the Zealots took their name, is characteristic of the Middle East and can easily degenerate into fanaticism. At first, the people supported Jesus enthusiastically. Later, they demanded his death sentence from Pilate. Such drastic changes can still be observed in this area of the world today. In this connection, we should recall a saying quoted by Matthew, who attached much significance to it: "His blood be on us and on our children" (27:25).

Pilate was an average Roman procurator. He was concerned about his career and, as chief of the army of occupation, he was carrying on a kind of "cold war" against the Jewish leaders. He was an anti-Semite and never pretended to be anything else. He was honest enough to see that Jesus was not a criminal but, on the other hand, he was not concerned enough to rally effectively to his defense. Basically, he was contemptuous of people, and attached no importance to human life. The case of Jesus was for him only another episode which he may very well have forgotten overnight. Herod Antipas, governor of Galilee — Jesus' own ruler — had come as a pilgrim to the festival in Jerusalem. He also may have been active behind the scenes during Jesus' trial, although the Gospels do not make this clear. Jesus once called him "a fox," and the Pharisees reported that he wanted to kill Jesus (Luke 13:31–32).

In the final analysis, everyone who had anything to do with the trial must share the guilt. Perhaps, however, we should draw a distinction between active and passive guilt, and be guided by the words spoken by the dying Jesus himself: "Father, forgive them; for they know not what they do" (Luke 23:34).

"...he (Pilate) brought Jesus out and sat down on the judgment seat at a place called The Pavement"

(John 19:13)

The Lithostratos and the Chapel of the Condemnation (left) are modern but beneath them can be discerned the foundations of the ancient fortress of Pilate's time. In Caesarea, a stone (right) bearing Pontius Pilate's name was found.

One of the outstanding relics of Herod's palace is the tower of Phasael, named for the king's brother.

CHAPTER 9 THE LAST DAYS

In which Jesus is arrested, tried and crucified

The Sanhedrin may have held its session in the house of Caiaphas or, possibly, in the great portico on the temple mount. According to ancient tradition, the proceedings before Pilate took place in the fortress of Antonia, which formed part of the barracks on the northern side of the temple and remains of which are still visible today. Nowadays, experts are inclined to think that it must have occurred in Herod's former palace by the Jaffa Gate. Here the Roman procurator resided whenever he came to Jerusalem from his official residence in Caesarea. This citadel on its high hill provided a good view of the whole city. In front of it was a paved square, officially called Lithostratos, where Pilate dispensed justice.

This was where the Way of the Cross actually began, but it is not possible to reconstruct the route in detail. As a warning to others, a convicted person was led briefly through the busiest streets. This necessitates making a distinction between the historically possible Way of the Cross and the one venerated in Christian devotion. The latter is based on an old tradition, dating from the

time of the Crusaders, and has been hallowed by the prayers of millions of religiously minded people. Weekly, on Fridays, the Stations of the Cross are still retraced along the Via Dolorosa and the pious tradition is revived anew. The temple area itself has no direct relationship with the Christian religion through association with Jesus, as it was considered defiled after its destruction by the Romans.

BEFORE ANNAS

After his arrest on the night of the Last Supper, Jesus was led through the Valley of Kidron, past the tombs of Zachariah, Hezir and Absalom, up the steps (traces of which are still in existence) to the city above. His destination was the western quarter (near the present Dormition Abbey) where the more wealthy citizens had their homes. He was taken into the house of Caiaphas, now commemorated by the Armenian chapel on Mount Zion. In accordance with true Oriental tradition, he was first of all introduced to Annas, Caiaphas' father-in-law and the head of the family. In the beginning, the investiga-

The palace of Herod, on the site of the old citadel, was most likely Pilate's Jerusalem residence. Remnants can still be seen near the Jaffa Gate in the western part of the Old City of Jerusalem.

tion was not official in form. Annas questioned him, perhaps in the presence of others, about his teaching and his disciples. Jesus answered, "Why do you ask me? Ask those who have heard me, what I said to them" (John 18:21).

One of the servants struck Jesus in the face, and he protested. He spent the night within the bounds of this house and it was in the courtyard there that Peter disclaimed his connection with him, in front of the domestics. This fulfilled a prediction by Jesus that Peter would disown him before the third crowing of the cock, which gives some indication of the time, since the period between 3 A.M. and sunrise is the time of cockcrow. In subsequent Christian imagery, this became a symbol of repentance. Peter left the place and wept by the wall. This is commemorated by the Church of St. Peter in Gallicantu (at cockcrow).

BEFORE THE SANHEDRIN

In the morning, Jesus was probably brought to the great portico to appear before the Sanhedrin, which had been summoned meanwhile. This body was the highest religious authority in the land, formed from three

197

"So they took Jesus, and he went out, bearing his own cross..." *(John 19:17)*

Thousands of pilgrims from all over the world take part in the Good Friday Procession, retracing Christ's footsteps (left).
The Third Station (right) marks Jesus' first fall.

separate groups: the high priests, the elders (mostly influential landowners) and the scribes (mostly Pharisees). The assembly was presided over by Caiaphas; it is not known whether he was wearing the official robes of office. The members sat in a semicircle on a dais. In front of them sat two court clerks. The place for the accused and for witnesses was in the center. There was no prosecutor in Jewish court procedure, his part being taken by the witnesses for the prosecution, and the evidence of at least two of these had to agree.

The testimony of the first witnesses was declared invalid. We know nothing of the details. Jesus was then accused of saying that he would destroy the temple built by human hands and erect another one in three days (Mark 14:56–59). This was a serious accusation, in view of the fact that the position of the temple was already being threatened by the increasing influence of the local synagogues and by the opposition of certain sects, for example, that of Qumran. However, this evidence was also rejected. Then an attempt was made to have Jesus admit that he was guilty. Caiaphas rose from his seat, and the

"...(there was) in the garden a new tomb where no one had ever been laid" *(John 19:41)*

The Church of the Holy Sepulchre is built on the traditional site of Christ's tomb. The present Basilica was erected by the Crusaders on foundations going back to the time of the Emperor Constantine.

whole assembly stood up also. He went up to Jesus and screamed, "Have you no answer to make? What is it that these men testify against you?" (Mark 14:60).

Jesus did not answer, and the trial seemed to have reached an impasse. Then Caiaphas asked the decisive question, "Are you the Christ, the Son of the Blessed?" (Mark 14:61). Until then Jesus had avoided referring to himself as the Messiah so as not to give the false impression that political intervention might be expected from him. Now he solemnly declared: "I am; and you will see the Son of man sitting at the right hand of Power, and coming with the clouds of heaven" (Mark 14:62).

Not only did Jesus give an affirmative answer, he also referred to his return in order to prove his divine identity. The simple "I am" carries within it the echo of God's own way of revealing himself to anyone who wishes to hear. To demonstrate that he was deeply grieved and annoyed, Caiaphas tore his clothes, as this claim to divine honor of being the Messiah was "blasphemy." None of those present realized the utter profound meaning of Jesus' mission as true Son of God. At that point, there was no need for further witnesses, for everyone had heard the "blasphemy." They agreed that Jesus deserved the death penalty. But that decision was strictly within the power of the Roman procurator. It did not amount to an official verdict.

BEFORE PILATE

As was customary, the crowd went to the Pretorium, Herod's splendid palace built on the site of the ancient citadel. Three massive towers still bear witness to its splendor. Pilate, who was familiar with Jewish customs, came out to meet them to keep them from entering, which would have been a transgression against Passover laws. The very first interchange reveals the tension existing between the Romans and the Jews: "What accusation do you bring against this man?" They answered, "If he were not an evildoer, we would not have handed him over." Pilate said to them, "Take him yourselves and judge him by your own law." The Jews said to him, "It is not lawful of us to condemn any man to death" (John 18:29–31).

"And when they came to the place which is called The Skull (Calvary), there they crucified him..." *(Luke 23:33)*

The accepted Holy Sepulchre (left) is an ancient Jewish tomb, but it has been enclosed in a modern chapel with a distinctive facade, marble pillars and columns. The lamps and candlesticks belong to the various Christian communities who worship here. On Calvary, the golden mosaic of the Latin chapel (below) represents the scene of the Crucifixion (Eleventh Station). The altar on the left, tended by the Greek Orthodox church, marks the place where Jesus' cross was fixed (Twelfth Station). In between (Thirteenth Station) stands the Latin altar of Stabat Mater ("Mother was Standing").

Various communities worship in the
Basilica of the Holy Sepulchre.
Among them are the
Armenians whose colorful service
in the church is pictured.

The Garden Tomb (below) is outside the walls of the old city of Jerusalem. Some Protestants view the Garden Tomb as the actual burial place of Jesus. The inner chamber of the Garden Tomb (right).

Then there followed the indictment: "We found this man perverting our nation, and forbidding us to give tribute to Caesar, and saying that he himself is Christ a king" (Luke 23:2). The religious accusations against him, which were decisive so far as the Jews were concerned, were not even mentioned. Instead, Jesus was presented as one rebelling against civil authority while the Jews adopted the role of protecting it. They made charges which, to some extent, were distortions of the truth. For instance, Jesus had never prompted anyone to refuse payment of taxes.

Pilate himself then questioned Jesus: "Are you the King of the Jews?" (John 18:33). To this Jesus answered, "My kingdom is not of this world.... You say that I am a king. For this I was born, and for this I have come into the world, to bear witness to the truth. Every one who is of the truth hears my voice" (John 18:36–37).

Jesus and Pilate: two worlds, each with its own, different truth! One is a prophet, speaking the divine word on his own authority; the other, a representative of the modern, liberal philosophy of life. Pilate

could not grasp what Jesus was saying. He was sure of one thing, however — the man was entirely harmless. "I find no crime in him." He really did not want to have anything to do with the trial and made several attempts to be rid of Jesus.

By chance, Herod Antipas from Galilee was in the city for the celebration. He was living near the present Western (Wailing) Wall in a Maccabean palace. In Byzantine times the Church of the Holy Wisdom would be built into this structure, perhaps to commemorate an hour during Good Friday. To get Herod's opinion, Pilate sent Jesus to him; this was also a friendly gesture on the part of Pilate, which served to relieve the tension existing between them. Jesus did not vouchsafe one single word to the ruler of his province. Herod had him dressed in a white cloak to make him look ridiculous, then sent him back to Pilate (Luke 23:8–12). The Roman soldiers gave him a great welcome, dressed him in a purple robe, and put a crown of thorns on his head (John 19:2–5). The common Middle Eastern custom of making fun of someone gains special significance in that it enacts all the particulars of the trial proceedings. The mocking irony indicated the people's judgments. Herod and the Jews made fun of Jesus as a would-be prophet, and the Romans made him an object of derision as a king. Jesus now looked pitiable, and Pilate displayed him to the crowd with the famous *"Ecce Homo."* Instead of laughing, the crowd answered with fanatical shouts, "Crucify him!" Annoyed, Pilate replied, "Take him yourselves and crucify him, for I find no crime in him" (John 19:6). It was then that the Jews finally revealed the real reason for their hostility. Jesus ought to die "because he has made himself the Son of God" (John 19:7). Jesus was interrogated for the second time. At first, he was silent and then answered by referring to Pilate's competence as a human being: "You would have no power over me unless it had been given you from above" (John 19:11). Jesus was referring to God-given authority. Pilate was confused by this appeal to his conscience. Then the people cried, "If you release this man, you are not Caesar's friend" (John 19:21). Finally, Pilate gave in. He climbed onto the tribunal and passed sentence: "You will be crucified." It was about the sixth hour on the day before Passover. The formalities were consistent with the usual manner of execution by the Romans, and thousands of Jews had already died in this fashion. Pilate made a demonstration of washing his hands, absolving himself from blame. But, Pilate was a Roman judge and, inevitably, had to bear full responsibility for the verdict. His action was, therefore, ironical, conforming with the incongruity which marked the whole process of the trial before Pilate. It focused on Jesus, and people made fun of him. This made the tragedy deeper and, at the same time, gave it a meaning which was more profound.

The site of these events was probably Lithostratos Square, an area on the Via Dolorosa paved with colored flagstones. The present site conveys a good idea of what it must have looked like, since the design on the pavement has not changed much. Though it goes back to a later time, it shows that the old techniques were still in use.

When sentence was passed, Jesus stood alone. His enemies, and even the law-breaker

Barabbas, had their supporters. Only Jesus, to whom all men were brothers, was on his own. This is a most moving picture, especially when seen against the background of foregoing events. His disciples had become fearful and scattered in all directions. In Gethsemane, Peter at least showed some courage by drawing his sword, but later he disowned his master. Nothing was told about the others, except Judas. Seized with remorse, he returned his betrayal fee and hanged himself. The money was later used to purchase a burial ground for strangers.

THE CRUCIFIXION

Sentence was carried out immediately. Jesus was bound naked to a pillar and flogged by Roman soldiers until, covered with blood, he collapsed. This moving scene must also be assessed in the light of its setting. That was the customary practice of cruelty toward prisoners. Jesus had to drain the bitter cup of defeat to the dregs. Then, he and two robbers were led by the squad to the place of execution. On the way, he was forced to carry the crossbeam of his cross. Meanwhile,

the upright post had been fixed in position.

The fourteen Stations of the Cross have historical foundations, all except the Sixth: Veronica wiping Jesus' face, which is legendary. Reaching the city gate, Jesus was exhausted and Simon of Cyrene — a farmer returning home from the fields to prepare for Passover — was forced by the soldiers to help Jesus carry the cross. Women lined the route. According to an old custom, they used to prepare an aromatic wine which would ease the pain of execution. When it was offered to Jesus, he declined to drink it, wishing to remain fully conscious while draining the cup of suffering. These womenfolk symbolize true humanity, illuminating somewhat the surrounding darkness.

The place of execution, Golgotha, meaning skull, derived its name from the shape of the rock in the vicinity. Jesus was made to lie on the ground with arms outstretched, prior to being nailed to the cross. Pegs were probably driven through the wrists before he was raised into an upright position. Then the feet were fastened. To prevent the body from breaking off under its own weight, it was

"were going to a village named Emmaus..." (Luke 24:13)

supported between the legs and below the feet. The early Church Fathers describe the crucified victims as if sitting on a throne. A board bearing in Aramaic, Latin and Greek script the words *"Jesus of Nazareth, the King of the Jews"* was fastened above the head. It was an ironic reference to the charge that Jesus had claimed to be a king.

The two robbers were also crucified. There were many people present, though not, of course, Pilate. A few soldiers represented law and order. It was their traditional right to divide the garments of the condemned.

Jesus' tunic was without seams, woven in one piece. It probably resembled a tallith, the Jewish prayer shawl. As duty bound him, Caiaphas was waiting for Jesus to make a confession so that he might absolve him. He waited in vain, however, and eventually left to attend divine services in honor of Passover.

Mockery and irony marked Jesus' last hours. The typically derisive exclamation "Aha!" (Mark 15:29) was part of it, as was also the sponge full of vinegar designated to keep him from losing consciousness until "Elijah will come to take him down" (Mark

After his resurrection, Jesus appeared to two of his disciples in a village called Emmaus. One tradition sites it sixty stadia (each 606 feet) from Jerusalem. Excavations have shown that this was a large Roman-Byzantine center with a "broadway" flanked by houses, wine and oil presses. The church pictured was built on the foundations of an old house, traditionally called the home of Cleophas, one of Christ's disciples who first saw him risen from the dead.

210

15:36). So, also, was the reference by the chief priests to his messianic mission, calling him "King of Israel" (Mark 15:32).

Throughout these somber hours, only a handful of his followers had remained — almost all of them women — comforting his mother. John, the favorite disciple, was the only one of the Twelve with them. From the cross, Jesus asked John to look after Mary in the future (John 19:26–27). Again, he demonstrated concern for his family. This is quite typical of the Jewish tradition which sees God as the father of the fatherless and the protector of widows (Psalm 68:5). The fact that Jesus, on the threshold of death, expressed anxiety about his mother, recommending her to the care of his favorite disciple, reflects his deep love and devotion to her. Finally, the last words of a dying man had special meaning. According to a widely held belief, those about to cross the threshold of death gain insights not granted to people during lifetime. Jesus' dying words are, thus, his last will left to his followers who cherished them and, in turn, passed them on faithfully. This is why his testament has special significance for all time.

Besides his words of commendation on behalf of his mother, Jesus spoke also of his tormentors, not to curse them, as was often the case under such circumstances, but to pray to God for forgiveness, excusing them of guilt because of their ignorance: "Father, forgive them; for they know not what they do" (Luke 23:34). Another word Jesus spoke to a fellow sufferer right beside him on a cross. This stranger had gradually gained confidence in Jesus, reproving the third victim for his outcries, then turning to Jesus with a heartfelt appeal: "Remember me when you come into your kingly power." The answer was, "Truly, I say to you, today you will be with me in Paradise" (Luke 23:39–43).

A further utterance of the dying Jesus was strange: "My God, my God, why hast thou foresaken me?" (Matthew 27:46). It sounds like a cry of despair but, in reality, Jesus was probably intoning a solemn prayer which began with these very same words (Psalm 22:1). It opens on a somber note, but gradually the hymn changes into one of triumph (at verse 22) and, in particular, to victory even after death, echoing the triumph of the

Suffering Servant of Yahweh in the prophecies (Isaiah 52:13–53:12). The implication was that Jesus' imminent death was not really the end.

Only once, through the long story of torment and loneliness, did Jesus complain in a most human way, "I thirst" (John 19:28). A little sour wine enabled Jesus also to speak his last words. After sipping a few drops, he cried out, "It is finished" (John 19:30). He was aware to the end of his God-given mission, acting on behalf of his Father, as he had insisted even at his *Bar Mitzvah* (Luke 2:49). Now, with assurance, he could go because he had been faithful to the will of his Father. His last words are, therefore, those of confidence and peace: "Then Jesus, crying with a loud voice, said, 'Father, into thy hands I commit my spirit!' And having said this, he breathed his last" (Luke 23:46). At the same hour, the Passover ceremonies had begun: lambs sacrificed and pilgrims beginning the evening prayer. In obedience to God, whom he called "Father," Jesus sacrificed himself for his people, to bring about peace among them. He died at about three o'clock in the afternoon.

Tradition holds that Christ, risen from the dead, had breakfast with his disciples. The traditional site of the place is in Tabgha Bay, now enclosed within the Church of the Primacy (right), where a rock (left) is shown as Mensa Christi ("Christ's Table"). Here also Peter was appointed to the leadership (primacy) of all other disciples of Christ with the words, "Feed my lambs... Tend my sheep."

214